Aries

Horoscope & Soul Guide for 2026

Monthly Guidance, Cosmic Rituals, and Rebirth Through the Stars

By
Lyra M. Rising

This book is a work of creative nonfiction and spiritual astrology. It is intended for personal insight and inspiration. It is not intended as a substitute for medical, legal, or financial advice.

Published in the United States

Table of Contents

Aries (March 21 - April 19)

Acknowledgments

This book would not have been possible without the constellation of souls who guided, witnessed, and believed in its unfolding.

To the Aries souls—fiery, fearless, ever-becoming—thank you for choosing to live with your heart unguarded and your courage unmatched. This guide was written for you, but also with you.

To the astrologers, teachers, and mystics—past and present—who have kept the wisdom of the stars alive: your voices echo through these pages.

To my editors, mentors, and creative collaborators, thank you for your clarity, patience, and fierce devotion to every detail. You helped shape this vision into something real and resonant.

To the unseen—my ancestors, guides, and guardians—thank you for every whisper of alignment, every nudge toward truth.

And to those walking beside me, in spirit or body: thank you for the quiet encouragement, the conversations at crossroads, and the unwavering presence when the fire dimmed.

This book is more than astrology. It's a mirror, a map, and a promise. Thank you for holding it with your hands—and your heart.

With gratitude and stardust,
Lyra M. Rising

Introduce

Welcome, Warrior: How to Use This Book

If you're holding this book, chances are you're ready to move with more purpose, passion, and planetary insight in 2026. Maybe you've had enough of vague horoscopes and scattered advice. Maybe you've noticed that life feels smoother when you align with cosmic timing—or more chaotic when you ignore it. Either way, welcome. You're in the right place.

This guide was written especially for *you*—a bold, brave Aries soul navigating love, career, and growth in a world that doesn't always match your fire. Whether you're new to astrology or have been following moon phases and Mercury retrogrades for years, this book offers a clear, empowering roadmap to help you thrive through every twist and turn of 2026.

Let's begin by exploring what this book is, how to use it, and why it can change the way you move through the year ahead.

What This Book Offers

"Aries Horoscope 2026" is more than a collection of predictions. Think of it as your cosmic calendar—a trusted friend whispering, "Now's the time," or, "Pause and reflect here," just when you need it most.

Each month features:

- A big-picture theme (to set the tone for your mindset)
- Forecasts in five key life areas: Career, Money, Love (Singles & Couples), and Health
- Special Advice (a mindset or action step that helps you rise)
- An *Astro Summary Box* with the most important timing cues, lucky days, and affirmations

Whether you read this cover to cover or skip ahead to your birthday month, you'll walk away with a clearer sense of:

- When to act and when to wait
- How to handle emotional highs and lows with strength
- What cosmic patterns are influencing your relationships, work, finances, and growth

This isn't a doom-and-gloom manual. Aries doesn't need fear—Aries needs fire and *focus.* You'll find both here.

Why Aries Energy Matters

Let's talk about you.

Aries energy is the spark, the starter, the warrior who rushes into new territory before the map is even drawn. You're ruled by Mars—the planet of action, courage, and independence. You're wired to initiate, to move boldly, and to speak up when others stay silent. In many ways, 2026 will ask you to *own* those qualities even more deeply.

But here's the twist: while your nature pushes forward, the planets don't always give the green light right away. Some months are about acceleration. Others are about reflection, restraint, or recovery. That's why tuning into astrological rhythms matters. It's not about controlling your fate—it's about *aligning* with the energies around you so that your effort lands powerfully.

Think of it like surfing. You could paddle hard at any time—but catching the right wave makes all the difference.

Sun Sign vs. Rising Sign: Which Should You Read?

Great question. Most people know their **sun sign**—in your case, Aries—which reflects your core identity, your ego, your drive. But your **rising sign** (also called your ascendant) shapes how life shows up on the surface. It governs your timing, your physical body, and the way other people perceive you.

Read both your Aries sun and rising sign chapters for the fullest picture.

Not sure what your rising sign is? You can calculate it using any free astrology app or website, as long as you know your birth time and location. If you're not sure, don't stress. Reading your Aries sun sign alone still gives you rich, relevant guidance.

In this book, we've written with the Aries sun in mind, but the timing cues—especially in career, love, and health—resonate powerfully for rising signs too.

The Planetary Map of 2026 (in Simple Terms)

You don't need to be an astrologer to use this book effectively. But knowing the *basic* rhythms that shape each year can help you make smarter choices. Here's a quick cheat sheet:

- **Retrogrades** = review, reflect, revise. Not ideal for launching or signing big contracts.
- **Eclipses** = turning points. Often dramatic. Excellent for releasing the past or initiating a big change.
- **New Moons** = seeding intentions. A fresh start energy.
- **Full Moons** = clarity and culmination. What's hidden comes to light.

We'll note these events in each monthly chapter and show you how they impact Aries energy specifically. Don't worry—we keep it all grounded and in plain English.

For example:

Mercury retrogrades in late April? That's a great time to clean up old projects, but not the best moment to launch a business. Mars entering Leo? Your confidence in love may hit a high around that time—use it.

By syncing your plans with these rhythms, you'll notice life begins to cooperate more. Or at the very least, you won't be caught off guard when delays or breakthroughs arise.

How to Navigate This Book Month by Month

This book is designed to be your monthly compass, not a one-time read. You can follow it like a calendar—checking in at the start of each new month—or flip ahead when you're planning something big. It's flexible by design, but powerful when used with intention.

Each month offers:

- A bold **theme** that captures the emotional and energetic focus

- Clear **forecasts** across five life areas: Career, Money, Love (Singles & Couples), and Health
- A special **action cue**—an insight or decision Aries should embrace
- A final **Astro Summary Box** with dates, lucky vibes, and key affirmations

You don't need to memorize everything. Just check the flow, spot the high points and caution zones, and use them to guide your choices. If one month feels especially intense or inspiring, return to that chapter as needed.

Think of this book like a toolkit, not a rulebook. The planets don't control you—but they do influence the "weather" around your choices. When you tune in, you can dress for the conditions and move with more clarity.

Tools That Help You Get the Most Out of This Book

To fully engage with the material and make it a useful part of your life, we recommend having three simple tools on hand:

1. A Journal or Notes App

Use it to write down your thoughts, monthly intentions, and any personal wins or lessons. Journaling keeps you connected to your growth while tracking patterns over time.

2. A Calendar or Planner

Mark the key dates suggested each month: lucky windows, retrogrades, or high-tension days. You can plan launches, conversations, or self-care days more wisely this way.

3. Your Inner Fire

This one's already in you. The courage to act, the strength to pause, the instinct to lead—this book will help you listen to your timing more clearly, but your decisions still come from within.

Understanding the Astro Summary Box

At the end of every monthly chapter, you'll find a boxed section highlighting:

- **Best Days Overall**
- **Most Stressful Days Overall**
- **Best Days for Love**
- **Best Days for Money**
- **Best Days for Career**
- **Lucky Color**
- **Affirmation for [Month]**

This is your quick-reference guide. Skim it at the start of each month, jot it into your planner, or screenshot it to keep handy. These insights help you time your actions with more flow and fewer surprises.

For example:
If March lists March 23–25 as high-energy for career moves, schedule your pitch or interview then.
If August warns of tension mid-month, you might avoid major decisions during that period.
It's not about fear—it's about *timing.*

A New Kind of Aries Horoscope

This isn't a generic forecast pulled from the stars and stamped with your name. It's written specifically for Aries energy—bold, brave, future-focused. But unlike a daily horoscope app or vague meme, this guide goes deeper into *context* and *clarity*.

You'll find:

- Themes that connect astrology with real-life decisions
- Clear interpretations of planetary shifts without jargon
- Focused advice, not fear-based warnings

If you've ever felt confused by phrases like "Venus in opposition" or "Mars square your 10th house," don't worry—we've translated those into plain, empowering guidance. You won't need to "speak astrology" to use this book.

Each chapter connects celestial patterns to what matters: your money, your health, your heart, and your growth.

Why Your Sun (and Rising) Sign Both Matter

This book is written with Aries **sun signs** in mind—meaning, people born when the Sun was in Aries. But your **rising sign** (the sign that was on the horizon at your birth) also plays a major role in how your astrology unfolds.

If you want deeper accuracy:

- **Read your Aries sun chapter** for identity and emotional insight
- **Read your rising sign's chapter** for life timing and external events

You can find your rising sign by entering your birth time and location into a free astrology site or app. Don't stress if you don't know it—your Aries sun sign chapter still holds powerful guidance.

One Last Reminder Before You Begin

This guide isn't here to predict every twist of 2026—it's here to *prepare* you for them. You'll face surprises, wins, slowdowns, and breakthroughs. Some months will push you to grow. Others will invite you to rest. That's the beauty of a full year lived in alignment.

You don't have to be perfect. You just have to be present.

When you meet each month with courage, curiosity, and a willingness to listen—both to the stars and yourself—you'll find your rhythm. And that rhythm? It's unstoppable.

Use It, Don't Just Read It

This guide is designed to be more than reading material—it's a tool. The real power comes when you interact with it. Let each chapter spark reflection, not just recognition. Astrology becomes transformational when you apply it to your decisions, rhythms, and mindset.

Instead of skimming and forgetting, treat each monthly chapter as a mini check-in with yourself. The insights you'll find aren't meant to dictate your life—they're here to deepen your awareness and sharpen your choices.

Simple Practices for Monthly Integration

To help you make the most of this book, here are a few grounding practices you can return to at the start and end of each month:

Beginning-of-Month Check-In

After reading the chapter:

- What's the theme of the month? How does it connect to your current life?
- What opportunities or warnings feel especially relevant?
- Which area of life (career, love, wellness, finances) deserves your main focus?
- What specific dates should you plan around?

Then, set one or two *intentions* that align with the forecast. Keep them clear and doable—things like, "Prioritize rest during the second week," or, "Speak up about what I want at work by the 20th."

End-of-Month Reflection

At month's end, look back:

- What unfolded as expected?
- What surprised you?
- How did your energy shift?
- What did you learn about yourself?

This monthly rhythm helps you build self-trust. The more you engage with the timing tools here, the more you'll spot patterns in your behavior and decisions. Over time, you'll begin to anticipate your growth cycles—and that's powerful.

Why We Include Rituals and Affirmations

Every Aries chapter ends with an affirmation and timing tips. These aren't fluff—they're tools that help anchor your focus.

Affirmations train the brain to expect strength and success. Even if it feels odd at first, speaking your monthly affirmation aloud—daily or during key transitions—can strengthen your mindset.

Examples include:

- *"I trust the timing of my growth."*
- *"My fire is focused. My path is clear."*
- *"I act with courage, not urgency."*

Rituals, whether simple or symbolic, signal that you're ready to shift something. Lighting a candle on a new moon. Cleaning your home before a big decision. Taking a long walk before journaling. These acts turn intention into action.

We keep things light and optional—no dogma, just support.

What Makes This Book Unique

If you've ever read a horoscope and felt like it could've been written for anyone, that won't happen here.

This book is written *for Aries energy*—for people who lead with fire, who prefer clarity to coddling, who want timing they can work with, not vague vibes.

You'll find:

- **No fear-based forecasting.** We don't do "bad luck." If something is challenging, we frame it as clarifying or transformative—with suggestions to navigate it.
- **Plain English astrology.** No jargon without explanation. If we mention a retrograde or eclipse, we explain what it means *for you.*
- **Empowerment, not dependency.** You don't need to check the stars for every move. This book teaches you to spot energetic windows—and then *choose* your actions with confidence.

Most of all, it honors Aries qualities: *initiative, courage, momentum, and independence.* Even when the guidance is to slow down or reflect, it's never about dimming your flame.

How to Use This Book Over Time

Start with the month you're in, or backtrack to see how recent events matched up. Some readers prefer to preview the next month's chapter at the end of each month. Others check in weekly.

There's no rigid system. This book is here to work with *your* style. Whether you journal every morning or just flip to the Astro Summary Box mid-month, you're still aligning with your energy.

And don't worry if you miss a month. Life happens. Just come back when you're ready—the sky will still be there, waiting.

Your Next Step

You've got your tools. You understand the layout. Now it's time to begin.

Flip to **January: Lighting the Match** when you're ready. Even if it's not January when you start this journey, that first chapter sets the tone for the kind of year you want to build.

And remember:

You're not following fate. You're partnering with it. You're not reacting to the stars. You're *responding with purpose.*

Let this book be your ally in doing what Aries does best—starting boldly, moving clearly, and staying true to your fire.

The Aries Blueprint: Traits, Strengths & 2026

What Makes Aries, Aries

Before we dive into the monthly terrain of 2026, we need to come home to your energetic roots. This chapter is your anchor, your blueprint. It's where we step back and ask: What does it mean to be Aries in a world that's constantly changing?

Aries is the first sign of the zodiac. The firestarter. The pioneer. The brave soul who says, "Let's go," before anyone else has even packed. Ruled by Mars, the planet of action, Aries energy is instinctual, bold, and unapologetically alive. You don't wait for permission. You *create* momentum. You *are* momentum.

And yet—there's more to your fire than just spark. Aries isn't just about starting. It's also about evolving. The astrology of 2026 invites you to refine your instincts, to wield your courage more strategically, and to channel your independence into lasting impact.

Let's begin with the core of who you are.

Strengths You Already Own

If you've ever been called "too much," "too fast," or "too intense,"—congratulations. You're living your Aries truth.

Here are the signature qualities that define you:

Initiative

You don't wait for the right conditions—you *create* them. You're a natural at launching projects, making the first move, and taking risks that scare others into silence.

Courage

Fear shows up for everyone—but Aries moves forward anyway. Whether it's asking for what you want or walking away when it's no longer right, your bravery sets you apart.

Honesty

What you see is what you say. Aries tends to value truth over politeness. You'd rather deal with discomfort than deal in pretense.

Independence

You're wired to lead, not follow. You trust your instincts more than the crowd—and that often puts you ahead of your time.

Energy

You have more stamina than most. When your heart's in it, you can outwork, outpace, and outlast. The key is keeping that energy aimed in the right direction.

These aren't just personality traits—they're superpowers. But every superpower needs guidance. Without grounding, Aries energy can burn hot—and burn out.

Your Growth Edge

Aries thrives when moving forward, but the real test of maturity is learning *how* and *when* to move. That's where your evolutionary journey begins.

Here are the patterns Aries must often work to balance:

Impulsiveness

Acting fast is your signature. But sometimes, fast becomes premature. The challenge? Learning to pause long enough to gather insight—*without* losing momentum.

Burnout

You go all-in. That's admirable—until your tank is empty and you keep pushing. 2026 will test your ability to rest without guilt and to build energy cycles that last.

Conflict Reactivity

Aries doesn't shy away from a fight. But not every battle needs your fire. Choose your causes wisely. Let others catch up before you rush to correct or confront.

Listening

Aries is direct and expressive. But sometimes, you miss what others *aren't* saying. Maturity means making space for silence, nuance, and emotional cues.

Interdependence

You value freedom. But the next level of leadership? Learning how to move *with* others, not just ahead of them. Power shared is power multiplied.

These themes aren't flaws—they're invitations. The more you understand the natural extremes of Aries energy, the better you can shape it with intention.

Aries Is More Than a Label

One of the biggest myths in astrology is that signs are static. But no, Aries is just "Aries." You're shaped by your chart, your choices, and your context. Still, the *archetype* of Aries—the bold beginner, the fearless leader, the warrior of truth—lives in you.

In mythology, Aries is often linked to the Ram—a creature that climbs impossible heights with sheer willpower. There's no path it won't take, no mountain it won't scale. That's you in motion: unstoppable, focused, and fierce.

But even the Ram learns. Even the pioneer learns to pace the journey, not just start it.

That's where 2026 begins—not with a sprint, but with a blueprint.

From Young Aries to Evolved Aries

Every sign has a growth arc—a path from its raw essence to its refined expression. Aries begins life as the spark: reactive, passionate, and proudly unfiltered. This early Aries stage is all impulse and instinct, like a child discovering their voice and testing the edges of the world.

But time teaches the fire to focus.

Here's how the Aries journey evolves:

Young Aries:

- Wants to *win*—often at any cost
- Rushes into action without a plan
- Reacts quickly, emotionally, and loudly

- Takes up space but doesn't always listen
- Fears slowing down (it feels like weakness)

Evolved Aries:

- Seeks meaningful *impact*, not just victory
- Understands timing, strategy, and patience
- Channels emotion into constructive leadership
- Uses voice *and* ears with equal power
- Knows when to wait, reflect, or let others lead

The difference isn't about changing who you are—it's about upgrading how your fire moves. In 2026, this evolution becomes especially relevant because the year's energy won't reward recklessness. It will reward *focused* fire. Let's explore why.

2026: The Year of Strategic Fire

While every year carries its astrological flavor, 2026 is uniquely impactful for Aries because of how the planetary movements intersect with your ruling energy. You're not just being nudged—you're being *shaped*.

Here are the major themes Aries will experience throughout the year:

Mars Cycles: Refining Your Drive

Mars, your planetary ruler, sets the tone for your stamina and motivation. In 2026, Mars travels through key zones of your chart, urging you to re-evaluate how you use your energy.

Expect:

- Bursts of confidence, especially during **Mars in Leo** and **Mars in Sagittarius** (great for bold moves)
- Caution and rest phases during **Mars retrograde** periods—where impulsive actions may backfire
- Opportunities to realign your ambitions, especially in career and leadership zones

This year, it's less about charging blindly. More about learning: *When is it worth the push? And when does power come from the pause?*

Eclipses: Bold Shifts, No Backtracking

Eclipses are cosmic resets. In 2026, they highlight areas tied to your identity, self-worth, and purpose. Expect pivotal moments—choices that close one door and open another.

Watch especially for:

- April and October's eclipses, which trigger shifts in your sense of "who I am" vs. "who I'm becoming"
- A need to shed outdated goals that no longer align with your true path

- Emotional intensity around belonging, leadership, or public image

Don't fear these shifts. They're not chaos—they're *clarity* in disguise.

Pluto & Saturn: Deep Maturation

Pluto's slow transit through Aquarius brings transformation to your long-term vision and how you relate to the collective. This isn't surface-level. It's structural.

Paired with Saturn's refining influence in Pisces, this combo helps Aries:

- Let go of lone-wolf behaviors that limit growth
- Build systems that support your independence without isolation
- Develop emotional resilience and spiritual stamina

Translation: less proving, more grounding. Less chasing, more choosing.

Core Themes for Aries in 2026

Pulling all of these cosmic threads together, here are the three main lessons the year offers Aries:

1. *Lead Strategically, Not Just Boldly*

You already know how to be first. In 2026, you're asked to become a *better* leader—not louder, not faster, but more intentional. This means managing energy, directing conflict, and building influence through collaboration.

2. *Balance Action with Reflection*

This year delivers moments that demand fast action—*and* ones that beg for stillness. Your task? Learn to tell the difference. Fire needs fuel, not just flame.

3. *Upgrade Your Definition of Power*

True Aries power isn't just in taking risks. It's in knowing what you *won't* chase. In 2026, confidence comes from discernment—not dominance.

Remember: you're not leaving your Aries identity behind. You're evolving it into something richer, wiser, and more enduring.

Aries Rising: Externalizing the Fire

While this guide is written for Aries sun signs, many readers will also have Aries as their **rising sign**—the zodiac sign that was rising on the eastern horizon at the moment of birth. If that's you, your Aries energy plays out more visibly in how you move through the world, your body language, and your instinctive approach to life's challenges.

For Aries rising:

- The monthly themes in this book are especially relevant to your **external world**—career, public image, physical energy, and daily environment.
- You may feel 2026's shifts more in real-time, as transits impact your **first house** of identity and action.
- When Mars changes signs, it can feel like your entire energy field is recalibrating—pay close attention to those dates.

Quick tip: combine this chapter's insights with your sun and moon sign for a more complete map. If you're an Aries rising with a Pisces sun, for example, your internal emotional world may need more fluidity than your outward Aries behavior lets on. Knowing this helps you lead yourself—and others—with more depth.

2026: Fire with Focus

So, what does it all add up to?

2026 isn't here to test your fire. It's here to *focus* on it.

You're not starting from scratch. You've already learned that speed without direction burns bridges. That raw drive without purpose creates fatigue. That passion without boundaries can become self-sabotage.

This year is about applying what you've learned. About stepping into the version of Aries that doesn't just launch—but leads. Doesn't just confront—but communicates. Doesn't just act—but *aligns*.

Here's what this year will ask from you:

- **Discernment** before decision
- **Reflection** before reaction
- **Directions** before driving

The opportunities are real—and so are the growth points. But with each bold choice, 2026 gives you a chance to step deeper into your power, your purpose, and your peace.

An Affirmation for Your Blueprint

Let's close this chapter with a statement to carry forward. Read it aloud. Write it down. Return to it when your energy scatters or your instincts feel foggy:

"I honor my fire by focusing it. I lead with clarity, act with purpose, and grow through reflection. I am not here to rush—I am here to rise."

This is the blueprint. This is the power you're building on.

Turn the page, Aries. Your journey through 2026 is just beginning.

January: Lighting the Match

The year begins with a flicker—not a flame. And for Aries, that's important.

You're used to starting fast. Charging ahead. Turning the page with a bang. But January 2026 asks for something different: clarity before combustion. Precision before passion. In the first few weeks of this new year, your job isn't to do everything—it's to do the *right* things at the right time.

This is the month of the *intentional spark*. There's power in starting slow and smart.

Overview Theme: Lighting the Match

Think of January like standing in a dark room with a match in your hand. You can strike it—but where will you aim the light? Before you set goals, before you take big action, this month invites you to **pause, scan the room, and name what you want**.

The astrological weather supports this approach. Mercury finishes its retrograde phase in early January, but its shadow lingers until mid-month. That means miscommunications, delays, or hesitation may trail into week two. Don't let that frustrate you—it's working in your favor. You're being given space to refine your direction.

Capricorn energy is also heavy this month, grounding your usual impulsive instincts. Instead of leaping into projects half-formed, you're asked to *build a foundation that can hold real weight.*

The spark is there. But the flame you're building? That's meant to last.

Life Area Forecasts

Career

January brings the slow return of momentum—but don't expect a straight launch on day one. With Mercury's post-retrograde shadow wrapping up around **January 11–12**, the first two weeks are better for *planning, organizing, and editing* than for bold moves.

Capricorn's influence supports structure. If you've been dreaming of a career shift or project launch, this is the time to outline your systems. Create your pitch deck. Draft the proposal. *Don't hit send until mid-month*, but use the early weeks to sharpen your strategy.

Around **January 18–20**, you may feel the green light energy kick in. Meetings align, people respond, and your sense of direction gets clearer. Trust it.

Power tip: *Set one concrete, measurable career goal for Q1. Make it specific, and let January be the month you gather the pieces to support it.*

Money

This month has a "review and reset" flavor when it comes to your finances. If the holidays left your wallet a little raw, don't panic. You're not being punished—you're being reminded to *align your spending with your actual values.*

The first half of the month is ideal for reviewing budgets, organizing taxes, or revisiting financial commitments. What's draining you? What's it worth? Take stock.

Expect smoother income or negotiation energy around **January 21–25**. If you're due for a raise conversation or want to discuss a new stream of revenue, late-month timing is best.

Power tip: *Avoid impulse purchases until Mars gains strength later in the month. Channel that restless energy into planning or saving.*

Love – Singles

Love doesn't start loud this month, and that's okay. The social energy stays a bit inward-focused until after the **January 20** mark. You may feel reflective, even quiet. That's not a red flag—it's a recalibration.

Use this early period to check in with your patterns. What kind of connections are you seeking in 2026? Are you swiping out of boredom or curiosity? Are you leading with your fire or guarding your heart?

Things lighten up mid-to-late month. Venus and Mars support social chemistry, especially after **January 23**. It's a good time to update your dating profile, say yes to a new invitation, or explore conversations with more confidence.

Power tip: *Flirting is fun—but clarity is better. Choose connections that support your growth, not just your ego.*

Love – Couples

If you're partnered, January starts with a subtle emotional fog. Not full-on conflict, but a feeling of "off-ness." Mercury's shadow phase may be stirring up minor misunderstandings, old patterns, or mismatched expectations—especially around shared goals, money, or long-term planning.

Don't let early tension make you question the foundation. Use the first two weeks to *observe more than you react*. Listen without interrupting. Clarify without accusing. By **January 15**, communication starts to flow more naturally, and the vibe lightens up.

Venus and Mars form supportive angles late in the month, making **January 23–28** a great window for deeper connection, physical intimacy, or a relationship reset. If things have been feeling distant, this is your moment to *reconnect—not by force, but by choice.*

Power tip: *Make one shared decision together this month—even something simple like planning a trip or a joint goal. It builds trust and reminds you you're a team.*

Health

Your physical energy may feel inconsistent in the first half of January—especially if you're still carrying mental clutter from 2025. This isn't laziness. It's your system asking for recalibration.

Aries often tries to "push through" fatigue. But this month is more about building sustainable rhythms than sprinting toward resolutions. Start small. Reboot your morning routine. Choose one wellness anchor (e.g., strength training, hydration, clean eating) and return to it consistently.

Sleep and digestion are especially sensitive until mid-month, so be mindful of caffeine, overstimulation, and screen time at night.

On an emotional level, clarity improves with *movement.* Walks, solo workouts, or even light stretching can help you release mental tension. Journaling after physical activity may bring surprising insight.

Power tip: *Let your wellness routine be a form of self-respect—not self-punishment.*

Special Advice: Don't Skip the Stillness

Aries doesn't love waiting. But waiting isn't always a weakness. This month, your superpower is *discernment*—the ability to pause long enough to sense what's real, what's right, and what's noise.

Instead of charging into a dozen half-baked resolutions, choose one *guiding word or phrase* for the year. Something that anchors you. Something that reminds you why you act—not just how.

Examples:

- *"Aligned action."*
- *"Bold with boundaries."*
- *"Make it matter."*

Write it down. Say it aloud. Let it filter your decisions all month.

Remember: You're not here to prove your power. You're here to *own* it. And in January, owning it means starting with clarity—not chaos.

Astro Summary Box

To close out the chapter, here's your quick-hit guidance for January. Pin it to your calendar, planner, or notes app:

Best Days Overall: January 18–20, January 24–26
Most Stressful Days Overall: January 3–5, January 9–10
Best Days for Love: January 23–28
Best Days for Money: January 21–25
Best Days for Career: January 18–20, January 30–31
Lucky Color: Deep Burgundy – for grounded passion and sharpened instincts

Affirmation for January:
"I act with purpose. I don't chase—I choose."

January Ritual: Spark with Intention

To work with January's energy—not against it—try a simple ritual that honors Aries' need for action while anchoring you in clarity. Think of it as lighting your match *with direction*, not just heat.

New Year Clarity Ritual
What you'll need:

- A quiet 20 minutes
- Pen and journal or paper
- A candle or small light source

- Your 2026 calendar (digital or paper)

Steps:

1. **Light your candle** and take three deep breaths. Let this small flame represent your inner fire: focused, contained, and intentional.
2. **Write down your guiding word or phrase** for 2026. Keep it simple, powerful, and emotionally resonant.
3. Underneath it, jot down:
   - One thing you're ready to *release* from 2025
   - One action you're committed to *begin* in January
   - One area you'll *focus on* without distraction
4. Then flip through your calendar and circle or highlight 2–3 power windows based on the "Best Days" listed earlier. Use those windows to schedule bold actions—meetings, launches, declarations.
5. Finally, read your affirmation aloud:
   "I act with purpose. I don't chase—I choose."

Let the candle burn for a few minutes while you sit in that energy.

Reminder: Rituals don't need to be mystical. They're just ways of helping you *remember yourself*.

Reflection Prompts for January

Writing it out is one of the best ways to align with your path. Use these prompts anytime this month when you feel scattered or stuck:

- What do I want to feel more of this year?
- Where do I tend to rush without checking in?
- What actions will help me *build* the life I want—not just talk about it?
- Where does clarity already exist that I've been avoiding?

Take five minutes. Let your instincts respond.

Final Words for January

This is your foundation month.

It may not feel as fast or fiery as you'd like—but that's the point. Aries isn't here to be reckless. You're here to be *revolutionary*. And revolutions don't always start with noise—they start with a decision.

January helps you decide where to aim your power.

So, take the pause. Claim your focus. Sharpen your tools. And when the spark catches, you'll be ready—not just to run, but to *rise.*

February: Courage in Close Quarters

Some kinds of bravery happen on the battlefield. Others happen in the bedroom, in the boardroom, or across the dinner table when you finally speak the truth that's been sitting on your heart.

February asks Aries to embrace a different kind of courage—the kind that doesn't come with a loud entrance or a dramatic win. Instead, it invites you into emotional intimacy, patience, and vulnerability. These aren't your usual comfort zones, but they are the heart of this month's astrology.

Whether you're navigating love, conflict, teamwork, or even your relationship with yourself, February is a masterclass in being real without being reckless. You're being called to deepen—not just act.

Overview Theme: Courage in Close Quarters

The astrological atmosphere of February pulls focus on relationships of all kinds. Venus (planet of love and harmony) and Mars (your ruling planet, ruler of passion and assertion) are moving through sensitive areas of your chart, urging you to explore how you give, receive, and negotiate intimacy.

This isn't just about romantic love. It's about emotional honesty across the board—family, close friends, collaborators, and even how you speak to yourself.

What complicates things: Aries is a sign that leads with action. You prefer doing to discussing. But this month, the deepest shifts won't come from what you initiate—they'll come from how present you are with the people closest to you.

In astrology, when planets activate "close quarters," it often means tight emotional spaces—those moments where you can't escape, avoid, or distract. You have to stay, listen, and engage with your full heart.

This isn't softness—it's strength, leveled up.

Life Area Forecasts

Career

February is less about grand leaps in your career and more about **how you work with others**. Whether you're collaborating on a team project, managing a tricky boss, or leading a creative group, your challenge this month is staying calm and communicative—even when your instincts want to take control.

Around **February 10–13**, workplace tension could spike, especially if expectations aren't communicated. Someone may challenge your leadership or your timing.

Before reacting, pause. The question to ask isn't, "How do I win this?" but, "How can we align?"

Things smooth out mid-month. By **February 14–18**, supportive aspects help you make progress through cooperation. It's an ideal window for strategic meetings, partnership discussions, or feedback sessions.

Power tip: *Leadership isn't domination. It's clarity plus compassion. Use both.*

Money

Money matters this month are subtly linked to your relationships. If you're partnered or share financial responsibilities with someone, expect money topics to surface—especially around **February 9–12**. One of you may be spending more freely, while the other wants to save. These differences aren't necessarily problems, but they need to be named.

Avoid big joint investments or shared purchases before **February 10**, unless you're both crystal clear on the plan. Later in the month, from **February 20–24**, financial energy stabilizes. This is a better time for renegotiating bills, subscriptions, or financial responsibilities in a way that supports mutual growth.

Power tip: *Money isn't just numbers—it reflects values. Talk about those openly.*

Love – Singles

Romance takes a nuanced turn this month. While February often gets hyped for Valentine's vibes, the truth for Aries is more layered. The first half of the month is inward-focused: it's about *you* understanding your patterns, your desires, and where you tend to settle or chase out of impulse.

Use the first 10–12 days to reflect. What kind of love do you crave this year? What dynamics are you ready to leave behind? This emotional clarity makes space for deeper chemistry—*not just attraction, but alignment.*

From **February 14** onward, sparks are likely. Mars and Venus offer bold, playful energy, especially in social settings or creative spaces. If someone new appears around this time, look for emotional intelligence—not just flirtation.

Power tip: *Connection is a mirror. Choose the ones that reflect your growth, not just your fire.*

Astro Summary Box: February at a Glance

To help you move through the month with clarity, here's your quick-reference guide to February's most important timing and energetic themes:

Best Days Overall: February 14–18**,** February 23–25
Most Stressful Days Overall: February 9–13, February 4–6
Best Days for Love: February 14, February 19–24
Best Days for Money: February 20–24
Best Days for Career: February 5–6, February 15–18
Lucky Color: Rosewood Red – for strength with softness and bold but grounded love

Affirmation for February:
"I open my heart without losing myself."

Ritual: The Brave Heart Mirror

Use this simple ritual to anchor yourself in emotional clarity and connection.

You'll need:

- A mirror
- 10 quiet minutes
- A pen and a journal

Steps:

1. Stand or sit in front of a mirror. Look into your own eyes. Stay there. Stay soft.
2. Say your February affirmation aloud:
   "I open my heart without losing myself."

3. Ask yourself (out loud or silently):
    - Where am I holding back out of fear?
    - Who needs to hear my truth this month?
    - How can I stay honest *and* kind?
4. Write whatever comes up in your journal—no editing, no judgment.

Return to this mirror ritual anytime you feel emotionally "off" or reactive. It's not about fixing anything—it's about *witnessing yourself with courage*.

Reflection Prompts for February

- When do I feel safest expressing vulnerability?
- What am I learning about the kind of love I want to give—and receive?
- How do I respond when I feel emotionally exposed?
- What does mature courage look like in my relationships right now?

Use these prompts to anchor your emotional growth throughout the month.

Final Words for February

This isn't a month for fast wins—it's a month for *deepening*. The kind of growth that happens not through force, but through presence.

You're learning to stay. To soften without losing strength. To open your heart without giving away your fire.

That's real Aries evolution.

Trust yourself. Trust your instincts. But also trust that closeness doesn't dilute you—it *develops* you.

March: Solar Power & Self-Renewal

Welcome to Aries Season. Your season.

March marks a return—not just of the Sun to your sign, but of *you* to yourself. After months of recalibration, emotional work, and inner untangling, you arrive at a threshold: the beginning of a new solar cycle. This is your invitation to *reclaim, restart, and rise*.

Aries is the first sign of the zodiac for a reason. You are the initiator, the spark, the leader who sets things in motion. And when the Sun returns to Aries, it reactivates your inner compass, illuminating where you've outgrown old patterns—and where you're ready to blaze ahead.

Overview Theme: Solar Power & Self-Renewal

The theme for March is **self-reinvention**. You're not being asked to tweak your habits or polish the edges. This is about **starting fresh from your core identity**—and making sure your outer world reflects that inner clarity.

The Sun enters Aries around **March 20**, kicking off your birthday season and re-energizing your first house of self, identity, and personal drive. Think of this as your cosmic reset button.

We also have a **New Moon in Aries** (likely between **March 22–24**), amplifying the urge to break old cycles and step into new intentions. This is an excellent time to ask:

- Who am I now?
- What do I want this year to mean?
- What am I no longer shrinking or apologizing for?

The energy this month is high-octane—but it's not about going fast for the sake of motion. It's about aligning with what matters. Your voice. Your goals. Your truth.

Life Area Forecasts

Career

Career energy lights up significantly in March, especially after the equinox around **March 20**. You'll feel a fresh sense of confidence and visibility—others notice your leadership, your bold ideas, and your willingness to take initiative.

If you've been planning to pitch a new concept, apply for a higher role, or launch a solo project, the window between **March 20–31** is ideal. People are more receptive to your vision, especially if you present it with clarity and emotional maturity.

Earlier in the month, there may be some fog or indecision. Use the first two weeks to review your goals, polish your pitch, and refine your message. **By March 18**, you'll feel a stronger pull to act—and when you do, it'll land with impact.

Power tip: *Let your actions speak louder than your ambition. Deliver, then dazzle.*

Money

This is a stabilizing month for finances. After the uncertainty of the last few months, March offers a clearer picture of what's working—and what needs restructuring.

You may feel drawn to spend on things that support your *independence*—think: business tools, coaching, personal branding, or fitness gear that boosts your confidence. These aren't indulgences—they're investments in your solar power.

After **March 23**, bold money moves feel more supported. Just be sure they're grounded in reality, not just impulse.

If you've been negotiating or reworking income streams, clarity should arrive by the last week of the month. Don't rush it—*timing matters more than speed right now.*

Power tip: *Spend where it expands you—not just where it distracts you.*

Love – Singles

When the Sun moves into your sign, your magnetic pull increases tenfold. People notice you. You walk into a room differently. You radiate "I know who I am"—and that's attractive.

That said, March is less about chasing chemistry and more about noticing *alignment*. Do the people entering your orbit respect your independence? Can they meet you at your level?

You'll likely feel flirty and confident from **March 21–29**, and that's a great time to say yes to new introductions, social outings, or reactivating dating apps—if you're doing it with intention, not boredom.

Early in the month (before the 15th), you may feel less socially inclined. That's okay. It's a prep period—a time to get clear on your values so you don't waste time chasing something that doesn't align.

Power tip: *Date like the main character you are. Not everyone deserves front-row seats.*

Love – Couples

March is a powerful month for couples—especially if the relationship is evolving. With the Sun in Aries lighting up identity and boundaries, you might feel a natural pull to reassert your needs. That's not selfish. That's essential.

In healthy relationships, this looks like recalibrating. You and your partner are renegotiating how you support one another's individuality while staying deeply connected. This could show up as:

- Rebalancing chores, decisions, or time together
- Making space for solo goals without guilt
- Initiating conversations about long-term direction

Watch for minor power struggles or moments of misalignment around **March 17–19**—especially if one of you feels overshadowed or unheard. Don't let small conflicts turn into larger dramas. What's needed is a conversation about *what's changing* within each of you.

Passion increases steadily after the New Moon around **March 22–24**. The energy becomes ripe for reconnection—physically, emotionally, and spiritually. Use this window to initiate intimacy or set a new shared intention for the relationship.

Power tip: *Let the fire you share be honest—not just hot. Truth builds trust.*

Health

Your physical energy gets a major boost this month—especially as the Sun returns to Aries and recharges your system. You may feel like you've snapped out of a fog. Your motivation, drive, and stamina come back online in a big way.

But here's the key: Don't burn it all in the first week of Aries season.

Sustainable energy will serve you more than adrenaline spikes. Focus on building strength, consistency, and balance. Think:

- Morning movement routines
- Strength training
- Balanced meals that support focus and mood
- Sleep rituals to match your rising momentum

The **equinox window (March 19–21)** is an ideal time for a personal "reset." You might feel called to do a spring detox, digital cleanse, or a deep home refresh—follow that instinct.

On a deeper level, March supports *identity healing*. Journaling, therapy, and body-based practices (like yoga or breathwork) will feel especially grounding. Don't just focus on how you *look*—check in with how you *feel* being in your body right now.

Power tip: *You don't have to feel "on" all the time to be powerful. Rest is part of your rhythm.*

Special Advice: Reclaim Your Narrative

This is your solar return season—your energetic birthday. Whether or not it's your actual birth date, Aries season marks your symbolic new year. Which means: *you get to decide what this next cycle is about.*

But first, you have to *release what's outdated.*

This month, take a moment to ask yourself:

- What parts of me have I been editing or shrinking to fit someone else's version of who I should be?
- What story am I tired of telling?
- Where do I want to be bolder—not just louder, but *braver*?

Then, take one symbolic action that reflects your return. It could be cutting your hair, changing your workspace, signing a contract, launching something public, or simply saying "no" to something that's been draining you.

Whatever it is—let it mark your re-entry into yourself.

Mantra: *"I choose myself, on purpose."*

Astro Summary Box: March at a Glance

Best Days Overall: March 20–24, March 27–30
Most Stressful Days Overall: March 16–18**,** March 5–6
Best Days for Love: March 22–24, March 25–29
Best Days for Money: March 23–26
Best Days for Career: March 20–21, **March 28–30**
Lucky Color: Electric Tangerine – to fuel self-expression, confidence, and fresh starts

Affirmation for March:
"I reclaim my power and rise on purpose."

Birthday Ritual: New Moon Rebirth

This month's **New Moon in Aries** (around **March 22–24**) is your most potent portal for personal reinvention. Use this window to set clear, bold intentions—not just for the month, but for the year ahead.

Suggested Ritual:

What You'll Need:

- A candle
- A pen and notebook
- A quiet moment for yourself

Steps:

1. Light your candle and take three deep breaths.
2. Reflect on the phrase: *"If I stopped hiding, I would..."*
3. Write down **three core intentions** for your next solar year. Think identity, purpose, love, and growth.
4. Then write **one action step** for each that you will begin this week.
5. Close by saying aloud:
   "I begin again, not from scratch—but from strength."

Let this ritual mark your *chosen emergence.*

Reflection Prompts for March

Use these to guide your journaling or meditation:

- Who am I becoming, and what do I need to leave behind to get there?
- Where have I handed away my power—consciously or unconsciously?
- What does self-leadership look like for me now?
- What would I do if I trusted my voice fully?

These prompts are especially useful around the equinox and New Moon.

Final Words for March

This is your season. Not just astrologically—but energetically.

The world doesn't need a version of you that's smaller, quieter, or easier to digest. It needs *your full fire*—grounded in self-respect, lit by purpose, and aimed toward what matters.

So take the lead. Take up space. Start what you've been postponing—not recklessly, but *reverently.*

You are not just here to try—you are here to *thrive.*

April: Time to Take the Lead

You've sparked your inner fire. You've returned to yourself. Now, it's time to *move.*

April isn't about dreaming, hesitating, or wondering if you're "ready." This is a month for bold decisions, career momentum, and powerful presence. The cosmic current is pushing you forward—and it wants you to meet it with vision and action.

Aries, this is *your* peak. Your ruling planet, Mars, supports movement. The Sun in your sign lights the way. And the lessons of the past few months? They've shaped you for this moment.

But here's the twist: leadership now requires more than fire. It needs *focus*. You're being called to rise with clarity, not chaos.

Overview Theme: Time to Take the Lead

If March was about self-renewal, April is about *self-direction*. Aries energy is front and center. Your courage, ideas, and instincts take the stage—and the universe is paying attention.

This is a month for:

- Owning your expertise

- Making the ask (for the job, the money, the visibility)
- Launching the thing you've been holding back
- Addressing procrastination and finally *acting*

But it's also a time for emotional maturity. Being a leader means not just speaking first—but listening well. Not just acting fast—but acting *well.*

Around **April 20**, an eclipse may trigger big shifts or truth bombs—especially around control, ambition, or identity. If something falls away, trust that it clears space for real authority.

This is the month to step forward—not just as a person with drive, but as someone others *trust to lead.*

Life Area Forecasts

Career

April brings one of the strongest professional surges of the year. You're not just thinking about what you want—you're ready to claim it.

The window between **April 4–17** is packed with momentum. Use it to:

- Schedule interviews or negotiations
- Pitch bold ideas
- Launch a new product, service, or personal brand

- Ask for a raise or promotion
- Step into a visible leadership role

Your confidence is magnetic, but remember: the most powerful leaders don't need to shout. This month teaches you how to channel authority without aggression. Think *decisiveness*, not dominance.

One watch-out: **April 20** may bring an eclipse (if present this year) that shifts career plans or challenges your assumptions about success. Don't resist it. What changes now is ultimately clearing a stuck spot.

Power tip: *Take the lead—but stay humble enough to learn as you go.*

Money

Finances get a powerful jolt this month—especially through efforts *you initiate*. If you've been considering raising your rates, starting a side hustle, or launching something solo, this is the time.

Income expands when you're clear, direct, and *know your worth*. And that includes saying "no" to lowball offers, draining commitments, or scarcity-based budgeting.

That said, **impulsiveness is your risk zone**. Around the eclipse (April 20), avoid risky spending or big financial decisions made under stress or ego. Slow down. Reassess.

Good money moves:

- Reinvest in tools that support long-term independence
- Audit your income streams—drop what's draining, double down on what's working
- Revisit savings goals and align them with your current values

Power tip: *Your power grows when your money habits match your vision—not your old fears.*

Love – Singles

With your energy shining bright, attraction is high—but so are your standards. And that's a good thing.

Between **April 12–21**, your charisma spikes. You may meet someone through work, a social event, or a bold move you take that naturally draws admiration. Just remember: leadership energy in dating is attractive *as long as it's balanced with curiosity*.

Watch for any tendency to dominate the dynamic—especially if you're used to calling the shots. Stay open. Stay curious. The right person won't dim your fire—but they also won't let you run the whole show.

Power tip: *Lead with confidence, but let connection be a dance—not a solo.*

Love – Couples

April offers momentum and motivation for couples—especially around teamwork, shared goals, and rekindled passion. If things have felt off-track or stagnant lately, this is the month to *realign* and move forward together.

Mid-month, especially around **April 13–18**, is ideal for serious conversations. Use this time to:

- Reassess shared priorities (money, time, long-term vision)
- Reestablish roles and responsibilities without blame
- Balance independence and connection more effectively

The energy is assertive, not sentimental—so don't expect softness at every turn. But that doesn't mean the connection can't deepen. Honesty and initiative will likely bring more emotional intimacy, especially when followed by action.

Watch for tension or power struggles leading into the **April 20** eclipse. Emotions may run high, especially if one person feels unseen or overpowered. If a conflict arises, remember: being right isn't the same as being close.

Later in the month, the vibe lightens. Chemistry flows more easily, especially when both partners feel respected and heard.

Power tip: *Being in love doesn't mean losing leadership—it means practicing it with presence and grace.*

Health

Your physical engine is revving high this month. With the Sun still in Aries for most of April—and Mars supporting your drive—this is an excellent time for strength-building, stamina work, and breaking through mental or physical barriers.

Think:

- Morning workouts that build consistency
- HIIT, weight training, or martial arts to match your fire
- Meal plans that fuel focus and endurance, not just speed

You'll likely feel bursts of productivity and mental clarity, especially during the first three weeks. Just remember: **momentum isn't limitless**. Burnout becomes a risk if you don't *pace* yourself.

Best practice: alternate high-output days with intentional rest. Don't skip recovery time. Your body needs fuel, hydration, and downtime to sustain your output.

Around the **April 20 eclipse**, take note of your body's signals. Restlessness, tension, or irritability could be signs of emotional overload. Grounding practices (like stretching, walks, or time offline) can restore calm.

Power tip: *True energy doesn't come from pushing harder—it comes from mastering your rhythm.*

Special Advice: Lead from the Inside Out

You're built to lead. That's not arrogance—it's Aries design. But the astrology of April reminds you that the *quality* of your leadership matters just as much as the quantity of your effort.

This month, your challenge is to:

- Step forward without bulldozing
- Ask for what you want *without apologizing*
- Say what you mean *without making others wrong*

If you've been procrastinating, hesitating, or "waiting for the right time" in any area—this is your cosmic nudge. Act now, or the opportunity may pass. Aries doesn't need to wait for permission—but it does need *alignment.*

Also, take time to ask:

- Where am I ready to step up with more maturity?
- Where do I mistake urgency for importance?
- What one area of my life needs my courage the most?

Let your instincts guide you—but let your *wisdom* steer the wheel.

Mantra: *"I lead with clarity, not control."*

Astro Summary Box: April at a Glance

Best Days Overall: April 6–10, April 13–18
Most Stressful Days Overall: April 4–5, April 20–22
Best Days for Love: April 14–18, April 25–27
Best Days for Money: April 8–12, April 23–26
Best Days for Career: April 7–10, April 17–18, April 28–29
Lucky Color: Crimson Gold – for boldness, earned recognition, and magnetic presence

Affirmation for April:
"I lead with clarity, not control."

Micro Ritual: Power Reset Practice

When life feels rushed or overwhelming this month, come back to your center with this quick reset:

What You Need:

- 5–7 minutes
- A quiet space
- Pen and paper (optional)

Steps:

1. Sit upright, place both feet on the ground, and take three full breaths.
2. Ask yourself:
    - "What am I forcing right now?"
    - "What is asking to flow instead?"
3. On paper or aloud, declare one aligned action you *will* take next.
4. Close your eyes and say:
   "I trust my timing. I lead with presence. My power is aligned."

This practice reconnects your instinct with intention—something Aries thrives on when grounded.

Reflection Prompts for April

- Where in my life have I been waiting when I could be leading?
- What does it mean to take up space with purpose, not pressure?
- How can I model clarity without rigidity?
- What am I ready to lead *and* let go of?

Use these prompts during the first and last weeks of the month for clarity and courage.

Final Words for April

This is your action month, Aries. Not for proving, not for pushing—but for *owning*.

The world sees you now. Your voice carries weight. Your ideas have traction. But it's up to you to lead that momentum with clarity—not just noise.

Trust your gut. Anchor your moves. Take the lead.

And when things get loud or heavy, remember: the strongest leaders know when to act, when to listen—and when to rest.

You've got this.

May: Pause with Purpose

After the ignition of the Aries season and the momentum of April, May arrives like a gentle hand on your shoulder: *slow down, check your direction, and realign your path before pushing forward.*

For Aries, this isn't always welcome news. You're a fire sign ruled by Mars—you crave movement, clarity, and results. But this month, Mercury retrograde slows your speech, tech, and plans—not to frustrate you, but to help you think differently. You're not being stopped. You're being sharpened.

Let this be your mantra for the month: *I slow down to realign.*

This is a cosmic editing season. Whether in relationships, career, money, or your internal world, May invites you to pause—not to second-guess, but to clean up what no longer supports your clarity. Consider it a breath between heartbeats, a moment of silence between movements.

The result? A wiser, more sustainable direction for the second half of your year.

Overview Theme: Pause with Purpose

The dominant energy this month is **Mercury retrograde**, which runs from **May 10 to May 28**.

During this period, the universe redirects your energy inward. Communication glitches, travel delays, or forgetful moments may arise—but instead of resisting them, ask: *What am I being shown about how I speak, think, and choose?*

This retrograde slows decision-making. It also encourages emotional truth-telling—especially to yourself.

Expect:

- Flashbacks to past relationships, goals, or habits
- Reassessment of your work-life balance
- A tug to simplify rather than amplify
- Emotional waves—especially if you've been ignoring burnout or people-pleasing tendencies

The purpose here is not punishment. It's *precision.*

You're not who you were in January. Your goals have evolved. Your confidence has grown. But some systems or habits haven't caught up. May gives you space to catch your soul up to your schedule.

Don't resist the slowdown. Respect it. Use it.

Life Area Forecasts

Career

Things may feel foggy at work early this month. Your usual Aries drive may clash with unclear communication, shifting schedules, or delays in plans. The culprit? **Mercury retrograde**, plus subtle internal resistance you haven't named yet.

Instead of charging ahead, try this:

- Revisit old drafts, strategies, or projects
- Reconnect with mentors, past collaborators, or unused ideas
- Reorganize your digital tools or workflow
- Review your public-facing work (socials, website, resume)

Avoid major launches or negotiations from **May 10–28**, unless necessary. If you must sign contracts, double-check every detail—then check again.

The **silver lining**? You gain clarity on what's truly worth pursuing. You might realize a goal you've been chasing no longer fits—or that a quieter opportunity is more aligned.

By **May 29 onward**, mental fog lifts. You'll know which doors to close and which to re-approach—with clarity and calm.

Power tip: *This isn't career stagnation. It's career curation.*

Money

Aries, you're bold with your goals—but May asks you to be just as bold with your boundaries. Especially financial ones.

Money slows this month, not necessarily in income, but in clarity. Impulse spending may spike during moments of emotional fatigue or boredom. Avoid online shopping black holes, quick buys, or overcommitting to things you *think* you "need."

Instead, use May to:

- Revisit your budget or subscription list
- Pause large purchases unless necessary
- Clarify your savings strategy or debt plan
- Audit what money decisions are emotionally driven vs. value-aligned

May 14–22 is particularly important: you may uncover a pattern around self-worth and spending. Do you spend to soothe? Delay asking for raises? Undervalue your time or skills?

This retrograde is a golden chance to reset your money mindset—and come out stronger by month's end.

Power tip: *Slow money isn't lost money. It's thoughtful wealth building.*

Love – Singles

If the past few months felt like a rush of bold flirtations or new beginnings, May arrives with a humbler agenda: *understanding your patterns*.

With Mercury retrograde in effect, dating may feel less electric and more introspective. Encounters may slow down. Communication may misfire. You might feel more inward than outgoing—and that's okay.

This is the month to:

- Reflect on past relationships, especially those that echo into your present
- Journal about what you want, vs. what you've been conditioned to seek
- Observe how quickly (or slowly) you let people in—and why

There's also a chance that someone from your past may resurface, particularly around **May 16–22**. Whether they reach out directly, show up in your dreams, or trigger a social media memory, take this as an emotional checkpoint—not a mandate to reconnect.

Ask: *Am I remembering connection, or craving familiarity?*

New relationships aren't off-limits, but they benefit from a slower pace and deeper curiosity. Let conversations breathe. Let attraction unfold. Don't rush into defining anything—May is better for observation than escalation.

Power tip: *This isn't a dating drought—it's emotional decluttering.*

Love – Couples

For couples, May brings opportunities for deeper intimacy—but only if you're willing to brave the fog of miscommunication first.

Mercury retrograde can cause crossed wires or minor emotional blowups, especially around everyday logistics, tone, or unspoken assumptions. What starts as "Where do you want to eat?" can escalate into "You never listen to me."

The solution? *Presence and patience.*

Slow the conversation down. Repeat back what you hear before reacting. Give your partner the benefit of the doubt—not as a favor, but as a strategy for a deeper connection.

Best use of the month:

- Talk about what's working and what's not—with curiosity, not criticism
- Schedule quiet time together (even 20-minute walks without phones)
- Revisit shared dreams: a trip you both want, a move, a long-term goal

There's a quiet kind of magic in May when couples allow themselves to reflect together. You may not "solve" anything, but you'll likely feel more *seen*—and that's worth everything.

By **May 28**, the static clears. You'll understand each other more clearly—and deeply—than before.

Power tip: *Connection isn't built on perfect communication, but on patient presence.*

Health

You've been on fire since the start of the year—but fire without rest burns out fast.

May calls attention to your nervous system. You may notice:

- Restless sleep or odd dreams
- Physical tension in the shoulders, neck, or jaw
- A desire to withdraw from overstimulation
- Emotional tiredness without a clear cause

This isn't failure—it's feedback.

Your body is telling you it needs restoration, not just maintenance. You've been *outputting* energy for months. Now it's time to recalibrate your *input*.

Suggestions for May:

- Build a tech-free hour into your evening
- Walk slowly (yes, slowly) and without your phone
- Try yin yoga, guided breathwork, or gentle stretching
- Embrace herbal teas, Epsom salt baths, and magnesium-rich foods

Also: don't skip meals or push through fatigue "for the grind." That kind of thinking leads to burnout by June. This is your chance to reset early.

By tending to your physical and emotional pace now, you protect your energy for the months ahead—when fire returns full force.

Power tip: *Rest isn't a reward—it's a requirement for your next rise.*

Astro Summary Box: May at a Glance

Best Days Overall: May 7–9, May 29–31
Most Stressful Days Overall: May 12–22, May 16
Best Days for Love: May 5, May 26–28
Best Days for Money: May 8–11
Best Days for Career: May 1–3, May 30–31
Lucky Color: Lavender Gray – softens urgency, supports clarity and calm

Affirmation for May:
"I slow down to realign. My stillness is strategic."

"Mental Detox" Ritual: Reclaim Your Inner Signal

When Mercury fogs your mind or your thoughts spiral, use this 10-minute practice to reset.

You'll Need:

- A quiet space
- A pen and notebook
- A timer (optional)

Steps:

1. Breathe deeply for one minute, eyes closed. Let your shoulders drop.
2. Write at the top of your page: *"What's draining me mentally right now?"*

3. Set a 5-minute timer. List *everything* that comes up—without editing.
4. Then write: *"What do I want to feel or focus on instead?"*
5. Circle one thing you *can* change this week (small is fine).
6. Close by whispering, *"I release what's noisy. I choose what's true."*

Repeat anytime Mercury retrograde feels overwhelming.

Journaling Prompts for May

Use these during slow mornings, new moon resets, or tech-free evenings:

- Where in my life am I moving out of habit, not intention?
- What pace truly nourishes me—and why do I resist it?
- What stories about productivity or speed am I ready to unlearn?
- What clarity is trying to reach me through the silence?

Even 10 minutes of writing can open surprising doors.

Final Words for May

Dear Aries: Your fire isn't going out—it's being redirected.

May isn't a "wasted" month. It's a wisdom month. The slowing, the silence, the revisiting of old thoughts or patterns—it's all part of your higher momentum. Your clarity is being fine-tuned. Your truth is becoming undeniable.

Let the world spin slower for a moment. Let your thoughts settle like sediment in still water. By month's end, you'll see what you couldn't when everything was moving too fast.

You're not behind. You're becoming more precise.

June: Refine & Realign

This month doesn't shout. It doesn't sprint. And it certainly doesn't reward impulsiveness.

Instead, June offers you the rarest kind of power: the power of **refinement**. Under the retrograde influence of Saturn and Pluto, the cosmic invitation is clear—*get honest, get real, and get aligned*. Not to impress others, but to honor yourself.

For Aries, this can feel uncomfortable. You're used to fire and forward motion. But now, the work isn't about speed. It's about structure. It's about shedding what's noisy or misaligned and building a deeper, stronger core—from the inside out.

Think of this month as a kind of spiritual editing room. You're not losing momentum. You're sharpening it. Quietly. Carefully. Deliberately.

Overview Theme: Refine & Realign

June's astrology calls for maturity—not the performative kind, but the kind that says: *I no longer chase what costs me my peace.* With **Saturn retrograde** (starting June 11) and **Pluto already in reverse**, the focus shifts to internal authority and emotional sovereignty.

What does that mean?

- You'll feel called to revisit the *why* behind your goals
- Old coping habits may resurface—but this time, you'll have the tools to respond differently
- Authority issues (with bosses, parents, systems, or even your inner critic) may flare up

This isn't a month for wild reinvention. It's a month for subtle, unshakable truth. You'll be guided to refine your boundaries, realign your vision, and commit to the long game.

Expect slow progress. Deep insights. And a quieter—but far more sustainable—sense of power.

Key reminder: *Lasting change isn't always dramatic. Often, it's quiet—but undeniable.*

Life Area Forecasts

Career

Work life slows down this month—but don't mistake that for failure. The *lack* of immediate results is your best ally in June.

Saturn retrograde wants you to examine the *foundation* beneath your ambition:

- Is your current work aligned with your purpose?
- Are you showing up as a leader, or burning out as a people-pleaser?

- Are your goals sustainable—or secretly exhausting?

From **June 12–18**, watch for moments of clarity or challenge. You may experience a reality check: a project delay, a moment of harsh feedback, or a wave of internal doubt. Instead of reacting, lean in. Ask: *What's this trying to show me?*

June is ideal for:

- Reworking long-term strategies
- Clarifying your leadership role or career mission
- Making quiet adjustments to structure, workflow, or client boundaries

Avoid launching major initiatives or changing jobs impulsively. The answers you need are still forming. Let them arrive naturally—without pushing.

Power tip: *This is your legacy season. Build it wisely, not quickly.*

Money

When it comes to finances, June presses pause—not to punish, but to help you reflect. Saturn and Pluto ask you to get radically honest about your relationship with money—not just how much you make, but how you value yourself.

Ask yourself:

- Where am I spending from fear, not intention?
- What do I avoid facing financially—and why?
- Am I undercharging, overgiving, or sabotaging my stability?

This isn't about restriction. It's about sovereignty.

Focus on:

- Tracking your spending honestly (no shame, just data)
- Reviewing past investments or financial decisions
- Setting boundaries with generosity—especially with friends or partners
- Getting clear on long-term financial goals that feel *anchored*, not impulsive

June 20–24 offers a supportive window for making grounded money decisions, especially around budgeting or setting up support systems (like an accountant, coach, or new tool).

Power tip: *Your financial future doesn't need fireworks. It needs focus.*

Love – Singles

June brings less flirtation, more introspection. If dating has felt exciting, spontaneous, or even chaotic earlier this year, this month shifts the energy toward *discernment*.

Under **Saturn retrograde**, the universe is asking you to raise your emotional standards. This doesn't mean becoming picky—it means becoming *precise*. Especially about your patterns, your self-worth, and your emotional availability.

If you're single, this month is less about meeting someone new and more about asking:

- Who do I attract—and what does that say about my beliefs around love?
- What do I keep recreating in relationships without realizing it?
- Am I dating with self-respect or self-abandonment?

There may be a temptation to reconnect with a familiar type or even an ex—particularly around **June 10–15**, when Venus aspects Saturn. If this happens, pause. Reflect. Don't rush to rekindle. Sometimes, the lesson is in the memory—not the reunion.

Use this quieter phase to rewire your romantic approach. That means deeper listening, slower unfolding, and making sure your desire for connection doesn't override your clarity.

Power tip: *Your standards are not too high—they're finally high enough.*

Love – Couples

For couples, June can feel like a bit of an emotional audit. Not because anything is "wrong," but because deeper truths want to surface—especially if you've been sweeping things under the rug.

Saturn and Pluto retrogrades amplify questions like:

- Are we growing together—or just managing routine?
- Is the emotional labor balanced?
- Where are we avoiding important conversations?

These aren't accusations. They're invitations.

June is ideal for:

- Talking openly about shared values, long-term dreams, and daily responsibilities
- Noticing how you both navigate stress, space, or silence
- Healing subtle resentments through honest (but kind) conversations

The energy around **June 18–22** may bring a breakthrough—or a moment of tension that becomes a breakthrough *if* you stay present. The key? Approach challenges like teammates, not opponents.

This isn't a month for grand romantic gestures. It's about intimacy that's built slowly—through trust, consistency, and clear communication.

Power tip: *Real love isn't always loud. Sometimes, it's the quiet work that changes everything.*

Health

June emphasizes inner stability over physical intensity. If your body's been asking for rest, reset, or recalibration—listen.

Aries tends to ignore early warning signs. But Saturn and Pluto slow things down enough for you to hear your system whispering before it screams.

This month, prioritize:

- Routine over radical shifts (e.g., consistent sleep, hydration, walks)
- Nervous system care: reduce digital overload, limit multitasking, say no more often
- Internal detox—not just food, but also content, news, and negative self-talk

You may feel more mentally tired than physically exhausted. That's a clue that your emotional load is heavy. Journaling, talking with a therapist, or clearing your calendar—even slightly—can help release pressure.

Also, avoid harsh cleanses or extreme workouts. Focus instead on movement that supports grounding (tai chi, Pilates, weights, or slow-flow yoga). Your body isn't asking to be "fixed"—it's asking to be *listened to*.

Power tip: *Balance isn't a luxury. This month, it's your medicine.*

Astro Summary Box: June at a Glance

Best Days Overall: June 7–9, June 24–26
Most Stressful Days Overall: June 12–18, June 20–22
Best Days for Love: June 10, June 19–21
Best Days for Money: June 4–6, June 24–27
Best Days for Career: June 5–8, June 29–30
Lucky Color: Slate Blue – steadiness, wisdom, and cool confidence

Affirmation for June:
"I choose integrity over urgency. I trust the wisdom of my pace."

Saturn Integration Ritual: "My Commitment Contract"

This ritual grounds your energy in sustainable self-leadership.

You'll Need:

- A pen and paper or a journal
- A quiet, comfortable place to sit for 20 minutes
- Optional: a small rock or object that symbolizes steadiness

Steps:

1. Breathe deeply for one minute, centering your focus.
2. On your paper, write:
    - "What am I committed to—even when it's not exciting?"
    - "Where have I avoided responsibility that now wants to be reclaimed?"
    - "What does mature self-respect look like for me this year?"
3. Answer slowly and honestly. Don't rush.
4. At the bottom of the page, write:
   "I am willing to show up for my evolution. One day, one choice, one breath at a time."
5. Fold the page and place your steady object on top. Let it serve as a visual anchor for the rest of June.

Repeat the affirmation during difficult moments:
"I choose alignment over urgency. I walk with purpose."

Journaling Prompts for June

Use these in small, quiet doses—no need to force long entries:

- What parts of my life feel solid—and where am I still pretending?
- What does success mean to me now, versus what it meant six months ago?
- Where am I being called to take fuller responsibility—and why does that scare me?
- What needs refining, not reinventing?

Answer one per week or return to your favorite whenever clarity feels far away.

Final Words for June

This month isn't about changing everything. It's about **changing what matters**.

The world might not notice your shifts right away. There might not be fireworks or applause. But you'll feel it. In the steadiness of your steps. In the way you speak, more gently to yourself. In the decisions that no longer need defending—because they're finally aligned.

Aries, this is your quiet revolution. A month of deep personal renovation. You're not crumbling. You're crystallizing. Let your inner structure evolve—so when fire returns, you'll have the strength to hold it.

July: Fire Rekindled

After the slow-burn recalibration of May and the deep restructuring of June, **July roars back to life**—and Aries, so do you.

This isn't just a return to movement. It's a **rebirth of momentum**. The fire that flickered is now a focused flame. The confidence that felt foggy is now crystal clear. Mars, your ruling planet, is picking up speed—and so are you.

But here's the key difference: You're not just acting for the sake of action anymore. You're choosing direction *before* ignition. You're not charging in blindly—you're aiming with intention.

This month isn't about making up for lost time. It's about moving forward **from alignment**, not adrenaline.

Overview Theme: Fire Rekindled

The cosmos supports a dynamic rise in energy this month. Mars is active in a compatible sign, giving you the green light to move forward—especially on projects, passions, and goals that had to simmer in the background over the past two months.

Expect:

- Reinvigorated clarity about what truly excites you

- Confidence in launching, leading, or creating
- An internal *yes* to being seen, heard, and respected

That said, there's a caution here: **don't overcorrect**. July is not an excuse to burn out in a frenzy of "doing." The real invitation is to use your fire **wisely**.

Key message: *The more focused your energy, the greater your impact.*

Life Area Forecasts

Career

July is a high-voltage career month for Aries. Whether you're aiming to step into a new role, pitch a bold idea, or finally make a move you've been dreaming about, the skies are giving you a signal: *go.*

From **July 8 onward**, you'll notice a surge in motivation and clarity. This is when forward action is most supported—especially in areas involving:

- Public visibility (launches, content, press)
- Leadership (team decisions, new initiatives)
- Independence (starting a business or redefining your voice at work)

If you've been waiting to pitch a project, make a bold career ask, or change how you show up professionally, this is your window. The clarity you gained in June helps you make moves that are both brave *and* smart.

Caution zone: **July 16–18** may bring tension, particularly if ego clashes arise. Be mindful of impulsivity or emotional reactivity in meetings, emails, or negotiations. You don't have to prove your power—**you are your power**.

Best use of the month:

- Pick one high-impact goal and give it your full attention
- Create systems to support your ambition (don't just wing it)
- Show up fully where you want to be seen—and stay consistent

Power tip: *Success doesn't just belong to the fastest—it belongs to the clearest.*

Money

Money flows more dynamically this month, particularly for Aries working independently, building a side income, or pivoting toward a more passion-aligned career.

July 14–21 is a strong window for:

- Smart investments (financial or energetic)

- Revisiting your pricing, income streams, or sales approach
- Aligning money decisions with long-term values, not short-term pressure

You may feel tempted to overspend on celebrating your return to action—travel, tech, experiences, or luxury items. While you deserve joy, keep your future vision in mind. Channel that fire into *wealth building*, not just momentary highs.

July rewards strategic ambition. Don't be afraid to negotiate, ask for what you're worth, or explore new earning pathways. What felt premature in May may now feel *perfectly timed.*

Power tip: *Money is energy—give it a clear direction, and it will follow.*

Love – Singles

Your romantic fire returns this month—and it's more self-aware than ever.

If June brought emotional reflection or reset, July invites you back into the arena of attraction with **clarity, courage, and playfulness**. The spark is back, and so is your confidence. But here's the shift: you're no longer willing to chase what doesn't see you.

Expect romantic chemistry to heat up around **July 10–20**, especially in social settings or through creative activities. Your magnetism is high. People notice you when you're in your element—especially when you're doing what lights you up.

But be mindful: not every spark is a sustainable flame. Fast connections may tempt you, but only slow connections will show you what's real. Before rushing ahead, ask:

- Do we share values—or just excitement?
- Am I leading with authenticity—or performance?
- Is this connection a mirror or a mask?

Use your fire to express, not to impress. July rewards Aries who date with **joy and discernment**. You don't have to protect your heart by holding back—you just need to *honor your standards*.

Power tip: *Flirt with freedom, commit with clarity.*

Love – Couples

If things have felt a bit heavy or distant recently, July brings a welcome shift: a chance to **reignite joy, sensuality, and shared adventure**. Not by fixing what's wrong—but by feeding what's *right*.

Your connection benefits from shared creativity. Think:

- Spontaneous getaways or date nights
- Building something together (home project, trip plan, even a playlist)
- Laughing on purpose—seriously, it's medicine

Between **July 11–13**, some tension may arise around independence. You or your partner might crave more space or personal time. Rather than resisting it, *respect it*. The more secure your bond, the more you can allow autonomy without fear.

This is a great month to ask:

- How do we support each other's growth?
- Where are we having fun—together and separately?
- What's one small ritual we can bring into our daily life that feels sacred or silly?

Aries couples thrive this month not through deep emotional talks, but through **action, humor, and shared passion**.

Power tip: *Healthy love lets both people shine—individually and together.*

Health

Your physical energy skyrockets this month—and while that's exciting, it can also be overwhelming if not managed wisely. After two months of internal work, your body is craving **motion, expression, and release**.

This is a fantastic time to:

- Start (or restart) a fitness goal
- Move your body outdoors—sunlight and fresh air amplify your mood
- Return to physical activities that *feel like joy*, not punishment

But be mindful: with fire surging back, it's easy to push too hard, too fast. Burnout is still possible if you ignore your need for rest, water, and consistency.

Signs to watch for:

- Irritability or restlessness when not physically engaged
- Skipping recovery days
- Over-relying on caffeine or adrenaline for momentum

Support your body by creating balance:

- Pair cardio with grounding breathwork
- Fuel workouts with whole foods, not just willpower
- Use movement as a form of emotional release—not distraction

By channeling your fire into **disciplined vitality**, you set yourself up for long-term strength and sustainable confidence.

Power tip: *Your body is not a machine—it's your ally. Train it with love.*

Astro Summary Box: July at a Glance

Best Days Overall: July 8–10, July 24–26
Most Stressful Days Overall: July 11–13, July 16–18
Best Days for Love: July 10, July 19–21
Best Days for Money: July 14–17, July 25–27
Best Days for Career: July 8–12, July 28–30
Lucky Color: Scarlet – symbolizes bold action, emotional truth, and creative leadership

Affirmation for July:
"My fire is focused. My purpose is clear. I rise with wisdom."

Creative Spark Ritual: Claiming Your Fire

Use this quick, energizing ritual when you're ready to move boldly—but intentionally.

You'll Need:

- A candle (any color, but red or orange is ideal)

- A mirror (small handheld or full-length)
- A quiet space for 10–15 minutes

Steps:

1. Light your candle and sit in front of the mirror. Look into your eyes.
2. Say out loud: *"I call back my fire. I lead with vision, not reaction."*
3. Breathe deeply, three times.
4. Speak (or write) your top goal for the month in one sentence.
5. Repeat: *"This is where I direct my power."*
6. End with: *"My fire creates, not destroys."*
7. Blow out the candle. Walk away with purpose.

Repeat weekly to refocus your energy.

Journaling Prompts for July

Answer with honesty, not perfection:

- What lights me up—and where have I been dimming it?
- Where am I ready to be *seen* more fully in my life?
- What risks feel *right* to take this month?
- How do I lead with courage *and* kindness?

Use these prompts before big decisions, during moments of doubt, or when you're craving creative clarity.

Final Words for July

Aries, this month marks a **turning point**. Not just in energy—but in *ownership*. You're no longer just reacting to life—you're directing it. The inner refinement of the past few months has given your fire a new clarity, a cleaner fuel.

Now, you're not just moving fast—you're moving *on purpose*.

Whether it's in love, work, creativity, or healing, July reminds you: your power doesn't come from force. It comes from focus. From direction. From truth.

Let this month be a celebration of how far you've come—and how intentionally you're moving forward.

August: Personal Power in Practice

This month, Aries, you step into the spotlight—not with force, but with **presence**. August asks you to embody everything you've been cultivating over the past several months: confidence, clarity, emotional maturity, and inner fire. It's time to *practice your power*—not in theory, but in how you move, speak, lead, and live.

We're deep into Leo season, a time ruled by the Sun—your fellow fire sign's domain. Here, courage isn't just instinctual; it's expressive. Power isn't just about action—it's about visibility. The real question becomes: *Are you willing to be seen fully for who you are?*

And just as you prepare to roar forward, **Mercury stations retrograde from August 5–28**, encouraging you to refine how you communicate, promote, and present yourself to the world. You're still allowed to shine—but this time, it's about **intentional radiance**.

Overview Theme: Personal Power in Practice

You've burned through uncertainty. You've paused. You've grown. Now comes the moment where Aries gets to express with confidence—but with a twist: *no proving required.*

True power this month is not loud—it's **aligned**. It shows up in:

- The courage to say “no” when something drains you
- The pride in completing something behind the scenes
- The confidence to speak without over-explaining
- The clarity to step back when your presence is enough

August invites you to be a **sovereign force**—magnetic, not because you push harder, but because you’ve learned to stand still and still be powerful.

The month will test how well you’ve integrated everything you’ve learned this year:

- Can you hold your ground without hardening?
- Can you be admired without losing humility?
- Can you shine without controlling the spotlight?

You’ll find that **people naturally gravitate toward you** now. That’s the reward of the Leo season. But what you do with that attention will shape how much of it is sustainable.

Key message: *“You don’t need to earn your power—it’s already yours. Now embody it.”*

Life Area Forecasts
Career

You're radiating leadership this month—and others see it, even if you don't. Whether you're building a personal brand, stepping into a role that requires more public presence, or simply feeling called to lead with more heart, August says: *Do it—but do it mindfully.*

August 1–10 is ideal for:

- Launching creative work
- Revamping your public profile or portfolio
- Speaking, teaching, or sharing your ideas in visible ways

This window is golden—**but be aware of Mercury retrograde**. Double-check your emails, contracts, or major announcements. Mercury's backward motion doesn't mean you can't move—it just means move with clarity and patience.

August 12–18 could stir up ego friction or power struggles in the workplace. You may feel tempted to prove your point or assert dominance. Instead, pause. Ask:

- Is this my pride or my purpose speaking?
- What outcome matters more: being right or being effective?

This is your chance to demonstrate *evolved* leadership: clear, calm, and anchored in truth—not drama.

Best use of the month:

- Refine your message before amplifying it
- Practice listening as a form of power
- Stay open to feedback—it may make your delivery stronger

Power tip: *True authority doesn't need applause—it builds trust.*

Money

August brings opportunities to **elevate your financial image**, refine your relationship with abundance, and claim your worth more visibly. Think of this month as a time to market—not just your work—but the *value behind your work.*

August 7–10 is a strong period for:

- Updating branding, bios, or digital storefronts
- Raising your rates or communicating your value more clearly
- Investing in tools that support your long-term visibility

But again, Mercury retrograde adds complexity. If signing contracts or launching major offers, consider:

- Reading fine print twice
- Having backup plans for tech or scheduling issues
- Avoiding rush decisions around loans or collaborations

Generosity is a theme this month—especially as Leo energy stirs the desire to give freely. That's beautiful—but beware of **overextension**. Support others, yes—but not at the expense of your reserves.

Questions to ask:

- Where do I equate visibility with overgiving?
- Am I managing my money in a way that reflects my current identity?

Money wants to flow where you feel **self-respecting**—not where you feel guilty or desperate.

Power tip: *You are your brand. Invest in it with wisdom and pride.*

Love – Singles

Aries, you're glowing—and people feel it. August stirs up bold chemistry and magnetic connections, especially for those of you who have been healing, evolving, or re-evaluating your worth in relationships. You're no longer just attractive—you're **anchored**, and that's irresistible.

Expect flirtation, fun, and admiration—especially around **August 9–13**, when both confidence and curiosity are high. Leo season gives you the green light to:

- Be seen without performing
- Speak your truth with playful ease
- Attract partners who value your joy, not just your intensity

But Mercury retrograde (August 5–28) reminds you: not every connection that starts fast will last. You may encounter exes, karmic loops, or attention that feels exciting—but hollow. These aren't setbacks. They're **tests of your self-honoring**.

Use your inner radar:

- Are they matching my energy—or mirroring it?
- Am I dating from a place of fullness—or proving I've still got it?

Real chemistry this month won't need to rush. It'll unfold in spaces of mutual creativity, emotional intelligence, and shared laughter.

Power tip: *Your glow doesn't need validation—it needs a witness who can hold it with care.*

Love – Couples

For Aries in relationships, August is an opportunity to reignite connection through **celebration, admiration, and play**. Leo season teaches that love isn't just about partnership—it's about recognizing each other's brilliance and making space for each other to shine.

The first two weeks of August favor:

- Shared adventures (travel, creative projects, physical experiences)
- Public affirmations (praising your partner in front of others)
- Rekindling romance with lightness, not pressure

August 12–18, however, can bring up subtle power dynamics. One of you may feel unseen, unappreciated, or left behind. These aren't signs of deep dysfunction—but cues to realign. Ask:

- Where am I withholding admiration?
- Are we leading together—or is one of us dominating?

Instead of competing, collaborate. Celebrate each other's individuality while nurturing your shared rhythm.

Couples who thrive this month will lean into **generosity**—not just materially, but emotionally. That means compliments, time, space, forgiveness, and enthusiasm for each other's wins.

Power tip: *Love grows when both people feel free to be fully expressed—and fully supported.*

Health

August brings a radiance boost for Aries—your confidence is rising, your physical vitality is improving, and your desire to take up space is returning. This is a fantastic month to **enhance your physical presence**, inside and out.

Areas to explore:

- A new fitness goal or creative movement practice
- Nutritional adjustments that support skin, digestion, and overall glow
- Body language awareness—how you *carry* yourself affects how you *feel*

But here's the catch: Leo season can trigger performance pressure. With Mercury retrograde active, it's easy to fall into over-editing your image or comparing your wellness journey to others.

Avoid these common pitfalls:

- Overtraining or pushing your body past its signals
- Using "self-care" as a mask for insecurity

- Projecting confidence externally while neglecting the rest internally

Balance is key. Movement should feel expressive, not compulsive. Diets should feel nourishing, not punishing. And your mirror should reflect pride—not perfectionism.

This is a good month to ask:

- Am I treating my body as a partner—or a project?
- What does **sovereign self-care** look like for me?

Power tip: *Your presence begins with your well-being. Shine from the inside, not just the outside.*

Astro Summary Box: August at a Glance

Best Days Overall: August 9–10, August 24–26
Most Stressful Days Overall: August 12–13, August 20–22
Best Days for Love: August 10, August 19–21
Best Days for Money: August 7–10, August 25–27
Best Days for Career: August 1–5, August 28–30
Lucky Color: Gold – Symbolizing solar strength, generosity, self-worth, and vibrant presence

Affirmation for August:
"I lead with joy. I express with power. My presence is a gift."

Ritual: Solar Sovereignty

A simple practice to embody your leadership, dignity, and joy each morning.

You'll Need:

- A gold or yellow object (jewelry, crystal, or even a sticky note)
- Mirror
- Quiet space + sunshine, if possible

Steps:

1. Stand tall in front of the mirror. Breathe deeply three times.
2. Hold your object and say aloud:
   "Today, I lead myself with joy. I express with love. I am enough."
3. Smile into your reflection—not a forced smile, but one of respect.
4. Commit to one action today that honors your truth.
5. Carry or wear your gold object as a reminder of your solar power.

Repeat this practice weekly to reconnect with your inner light and embodied self-worth.

Journaling Prompts for August

Use these to realign your voice, value, and visibility:

- Where in my life am I shrinking out of habit—not truth?
- What does *healthy pride* look like for me?
- How do I want to be seen—and what am I ready to stop hiding?
- In what spaces do I feel powerful yet playful? How can I spend more time there?

Let these prompts guide mid-month reflections, especially around Mercury retrograde moments.

Final Words for August

This is the month you stop chasing—and start *glowing*.

You've earned your clarity. You've cultivated your power. Now, August invites you to **wear it well**. Not for applause. Not to dominate. But to lead, to love, and to live from your core truth.

Your voice is valuable. Your joy is medicine. Your presence is needed.

Let this chapter be your turning point: from fire to flame bearer, from solo warrior to heart-led leader. And as Mercury helps you refine your message, remember—true power doesn't shout. It resonates.

September: Harvesting Wisdom

Welcome to Virgo season, Aries—a time to trade speed for structure, flash for focus, and passion for precision.

After the bold outward expression of July and August, September arrives like a cool, steady breath. This is not a month for dramatic moves or reinvention. It's for cleaning up, refining, and **making peace with the process**.

Think of it as a cosmic harvest: you've planted bold intentions, clarified your desires, and taken courageous steps. Now comes the part where you **integrate your growth**, edit what's no longer aligned, and build sustainable systems for what's next.

Virgo energy isn't always glamorous—but it is deeply **empowering**. It helps you find confidence in clarity, strength in simplicity, and pride in the behind-the-scenes work.

This month, Mercury—your planetary guide through Virgo—**goes direct on September 15**, ending a retrograde that may have fogged up communication or decision-making. Once it clears, a New Moon arrives with a powerful reset.

The message? *Structure sets you free.*

Overview Theme: Harvesting Wisdom

September teaches you to move differently.

Instead of asking, "What else can I do?"
Ask, "How can I do what I'm already doing better?"

Instead of charging forward, Virgo says:
"Pause. Observe. Tweak. Simplify."

This is the art of **refinement**, and it matters more than you think.

Expect a strong pull to:

- Reorganize your calendar, space, or systems
- Create new health or work routines
- Set (and enforce) clearer boundaries in relationships
- Reflect on what's working—and remove what's not

This energy may feel boring or restrictive at first, especially for fast-moving Aries. But here's the truth: Virgo doesn't slow you down to stop you. It slows you down to **align you**.

Don't resist the slower pace. Embrace it. The stillness is fertile ground.

Key message: *"Discipline isn't a cage. It's the container for your freedom."*

Life Area Forecasts

Career

September isn't a launch month—it's a **fine-tuning month**.

This is the perfect time to:

- Refine your message, mission, or methods
- Organize your workspace, calendar, or client flow
- Edit content, systems, or offers that feel outdated

If you've been scattered or stretched thin, Virgo energy helps you **streamline and systematize**. Instead of trying to do more, focus on doing **less—but better**.

You may feel a pull toward delegation, restructuring your workflow, or reevaluating how you use your time each day. These nudges aren't distractions—they're *evolution cues*.

Mercury stations direct on September 15, clearing communication blocks and helping you move forward with clarity. The **Virgo New Moon on September 17** is a beautiful portal to set grounded intentions for your work life—intentions rooted in quality, not hustle.

Best use of the month:

- Create structure for your creative energy
- Set clearer boundaries with clients, bosses, or collaborators
- Shift from reactive work to proactive planning

Power tip: *True impact isn't measured by chaos—it's built in quiet consistency.*

Money

This is a financial planning month—not a splurge month.

Virgo's earthy influence encourages **budgeting, review, and reallocation**. You're not being asked to cut corners—but to align your spending and saving with your *true values*.

Focus on:

- Reassessing subscriptions, expenses, or services that no longer serve you
- Creating a better system for tracking income, outflow, or savings
- Simplifying your approach to money—clarity breeds confidence

September 7–10 is a good window to audit or revisit financial goals, while **September 18–22** supports restructured approaches to pricing, offerings, or income streams.

The money wisdom of Virgo? *Sustainability > quick wins.*

Ask yourself:

- Where am I spending energy (or money) that doesn't feed me back?
- What does "financial integrity" mean for me now?
- Is my money aligned with how I want to feel—not just what I want to have?

Power tip: *Money grows best in organized, intentional soil.*

Love – Singles

In September, your romantic life slows down—but this is a gift, not a setback. With Virgo season in full effect and Mercury retrograde through mid-month, the cosmos encourages you to **refine your relationship standards** and listen more closely to your intuition than your impulses.

This month isn't about the thrill of the chase. It's about clarity:

- What kind of connection do you want?

- Where are your relationship patterns ready for revision?
- How can you lead with honesty—especially with yourself?

If you meet someone new during this time, especially before **September 15**, take things slow. First impressions may be incomplete or misread due to the retrograde. But don't write someone off too quickly either—clarity builds gradually.

This is also a powerful time to:

- Journal about past relationship lessons
- Revisit an old flame (emotionally, not literally) to see what still holds true
- Edit your dating profile or clarify your communication style

Romantic magic isn't gone—it's just *quieter*. Virgo invites you to build connections like gardens: with care, patience, and pruning where needed.

Power tip: *Long-term love starts with short-term honesty.*

Love – Couples

For those in relationships, September asks for **shared structure, mutual support, and real-world love**. This isn't a month of romantic grand gestures—it's a time for logistical syncing, small acts of service, and thoughtful attention to the details that keep love strong.

Themes you may encounter:

- Revisiting shared routines or schedules
- Clarifying boundaries around personal time, chores, or digital habits
- Supporting each other's health or wellness goals

Around **September 13–17**, emotional misunderstandings are possible, especially if one partner is craving more space or organization and the other feels criticized. Instead of jumping to conclusions, practice curiosity:

- "What would make things feel smoother for both of us?"
- "How can we show up better for each other this week?"
- "Are we assuming—or communicating?"

The beauty of Virgo energy is its commitment to *real care*. It doesn't dazzle—it nurtures. If you're willing to tend to the unsexy parts of love, you'll emerge feeling more connected, more grounded, and more respected.

Power tip: *In love, details matter. Don't underestimate the power of showing up on time, listening fully, or making their coffee just the way they like it.*

Health

This is your **wellness month, Aries**—but not the "bootcamp and green juice" kind (unless that feels joyful). September offers a deeper, more sustainable approach: realigning with your body's needs through presence, routine, and gentle course correction.

Virgo rules digestion, nervous system balance, and daily rituals. Pay attention to:

- Gut health, food sensitivity, and hydration
- Sleep quality and screen-time boundaries
- Whether your current habits match your energy needs

Instead of overhauling everything, try this:

1. Choose one small upgrade per week (e.g., drink more water, stretch every morning).
2. Track how it impacts your mood, clarity, or energy.
3. Build consistency through compassion, not pressure.

Between September 5–15, you may feel more sensitive to stress, overstimulation, or schedule disruptions. Use this period to re-establish healthy rhythms, not to prove anything.

This is also a beautiful time to declutter—both physically and digitally. Virgo healing thrives on **order, space, and simplicity**. Think of it as a nervous system detox.

Power tip: *Wellness isn't a sprint—it's the rhythm you return to when the world gets loud.*

Astro Summary Box: September at a Glance

Best Days Overall: September 5–7, September 17–20
Most Stressful Days Overall: September 12–13, September 22–24
Best Days for Love: September 6, September 25
Best Days for Money: September 10–11, September 26–28
Best Days for Career: September 15, September 19–20
Lucky Color: Earth green – Symbolizing grounded wisdom, sustainable growth, and sacred structure

Affirmation for September:
"I refine with purpose. I root my power in clarity. Simplicity is my strength."

Ritual: Sacred Systems Reset

Virgo season is ideal for ritualizing order—not just for productivity, but for peace.

You'll Need:

- A blank journal page or digital planner
- 1 candle (green or white)
- 20 minutes of focused space

Steps:

1. Light your candle. Take three grounding breaths.
2. Write three areas of your life that feel scattered or disorganized (e.g., time, finances, self-care).
3. For each area, write one small shift or boundary you could implement this month.
4. Commit to a "sacred reset day" weekly—time to review, realign, and clear mental clutter.
5. Close by writing this at the bottom of the page: *"I create systems that honor my energy and expand my freedom."*

Keep this page visible throughout the month. Let it become a map back to ease.

Journaling Prompts for September

- What routines genuinely support me—and which ones drain me?
- Where have I been confusing busy with aligned?
- What would it feel like to create from stillness instead of stress?
- What does *enough* mean to me now?

Use these to guide your weekly reviews or moments of overwhelm.

Final Words for September

Aries, your fire still burns—but this month, it warms rather than scorches.

September teaches you that mastery isn't about momentum—it's about alignment. The most powerful move you can make right now isn't to charge ahead. It's to pause, refine, and root down.

Let this be the chapter where you trade chaos for clarity. Let systems serve you. Let boundaries support you. Let simplicity restore you.

There is strength in stillness. There is wisdom in the work no one sees.

Let Virgo season anchor you—and prepare you for the transformation that's coming next.

October: Eclipse Crossroads

October doesn't whisper—it roars. For Aries, this is not just another month—it's a **turning point**. Two eclipses—**a Solar Eclipse in Libra on October 2** and **a Lunar Eclipse in Aries on October 17**—form a powerful corridor of transformation. This is a rare cosmic invitation to examine what's working, what's not, and most importantly, *who you are becoming.*

Eclipses are not "bad omens"—but they are disruptive by design. They reveal what's hidden and remove what no longer serves. For Aries, this month activates your identity, partnerships, and purpose. It's not about tweaking at the edges. It's about **releasing an outdated version of you** so something more aligned can take root.

This chapter is about **crossroads energy**—those moments when you feel pulled between safety and growth, between loyalty and liberation. October won't let you stay where you've been. It asks for bravery, not busyness. For presence, not performance.

And as an Aries, this is your sacred fire: to **initiate transformation**, even when it means facing discomfort.

Overview Theme: Eclipse Crossroads

There are years when everything flows. Then some months *change everything.*

October is the latter.

The **Libra Solar Eclipse on October 2** brings a sudden shake-up to your relationships, contracts, and commitments. Expect insights or events that highlight where you've over-compromised, where balance has become imbalance, and where you need to reclaim your voice. This energy may feel jarring—but also clarifying.

Two weeks later, the **Aries Lunar Eclipse on October 17** turns the spotlight inward. This is your personal Full Moon eclipse—a powerful release point that marks the end of an identity cycle that began 18 months ago. It's not just about letting go of roles, labels, or relationships—it's about **releasing who you thought you had to be**.

Eclipses move in six-month storylines. Look back to **April 2025** (Aries Solar Eclipse) for clues about what's now culminating, ending, or transforming.

This is a time of:

- Sudden clarity
- Necessary goodbyes

- Emotional release
- Identity breakthroughs

Don't try to "solve" everything. October is not linear—it's **liminal**. It's the space between what was and what will be.

Your job is not to control—but to respond with courage.

Life Area Forecasts

Career

Career matters may feel unstable—but that's not a sign of failure. It's a **cosmic shake-up** meant to realign you with your true path.

The **October 2 Solar Eclipse** could bring:

- An unexpected shift in leadership, clients, or roles
- A revelation that something you've committed to no longer fits
- A contract ending—or a powerful new offer that challenges your comfort zone

If something suddenly falls away, don't rush to replace it. Sit with the space. October gives you room to reconnect with your *why*.

Then, the **Aries Lunar Eclipse on October 17** turns inward:

- Is the career path you're on a true reflection of who you are now?
- Are you leading—or people-pleasing?
- Are you motivated by purpose—or proving yourself?

This is the moment to step into authentic power. Not the flashy kind, but the kind that says: *"This is who I am. This is what I stand for."*

Power Tip: If something leaves your career sphere this month, it's not rejection—it's *release*. Trust what clears. Trust what calls.

Money

Financial energy this month is tied to **value, power, and shared resources**.

With Libra and Aries ruling the axis of self and others, money becomes a mirror:

- Are you overgiving or undercharging in your work or relationships?
- Are you financially dependent on something that no longer feels secure?
- Are you willing to re-negotiate the energetic and financial terms of your life?

Between the eclipses, **October 10–19**, there may be pressure or conflict around joint accounts, investments, or even inheritance matters. If you're in business partnerships, contracts may shift or dissolve. Stay calm. Be clear. Avoid impulsive moves.

Instead, use this month to:

- Review your financial boundaries
- Assess where your time/energy is under-compensated
- Ask yourself: *"What is my time worth?"*

By month's end, a new income path may begin to emerge—one more aligned with your **authentic identity**, not your old survival strategies.

Power Tip: Money that costs you your peace isn't abundance. Reclaim your worth.

Love – Singles

For single Aries, October's eclipses are a **truth serum** for your heart.

The **Libra Solar Eclipse on October 2** may spotlight how you show up in partnerships—or why certain connections haven't lasted. You might realize you've been overcompromising, ignoring red flags, or holding onto an old romantic identity that no longer reflects your current self.

Between October 2–15, karmic connections could appear or reappear. These encounters aren't necessarily "forever people"—they're mirrors, showing you something about your patterns, desires, and boundaries. Some may feel intense but short-lived, while others could spark deep soul recognition.

The **Aries Lunar Eclipse on October 17** turns the focus inward:

- What do you want in love, stripped of societal or family expectations?
- Are you dating from a place of wholeness, or to fill a gap?
- Where are you ready to choose yourself over the idea of "us"?

You may find yourself walking away from situations that are "almost right" but not fully aligned. This is your love reset.

Power Tip: The right person won't dim your fire—they'll help you tend it.

Love – Couples

For couples, October is a relationship turning point.

The **October 2 Solar Eclipse** in your partnership sector can shake up dynamics:

- Relationship agreements may be tested or renegotiated
- Old unresolved issues could resurface suddenly
- You may need to face hard truths about reciprocity, respect, or shared vision

Some Aries will decide to deepen commitment—others may realize it's time to part ways. This isn't about punishment—it's about alignment.

The **October 17 Lunar Eclipse** in your sign turns the mirror back on you:

- Are you showing up authentically in the relationship?
- Are you honoring your needs while honoring your partner's?
- Have you been hiding parts of yourself to "keep the peace"?

Eclipses don't always end relationships, but they do demand **evolution**. For couples willing to grow together, October can be a breakthrough month for intimacy, honesty, and mutual respect.

Power Tip: In love, the truth will either set you free together—or set you free apart.

Health

Eclipse season can be intense—not just emotionally, but physically. Your body processes change as much as your mind does.

During October:

- Energy levels may fluctuate dramatically
- Sleep patterns may be disrupted by vivid dreams or restlessness
- Your nervous system could feel more sensitive to stress

Support your health by **slowing down between eclipses (October 2–17)**:

- Prioritize grounding practices (nature walks, yoga, journaling)
- Drink more water than usual—eclipses can be dehydrating on an energetic level
- Eat grounding foods (root vegetables, warm meals) to help you feel stable

This is also a good month for **emotional detox**. Cry if you need to. Rest when your body asks. Release tension through movement or creative expression.

Remember: Transformation is demanding work. Even when it's invisible, your system is processing deeply.

Power Tip: Your body is your anchor—tend to it with devotion.

Astro Summary Box: October at a Glance

Best Days Overall: October 5–6, October 20–22
Most Stressful Days Overall: October 2, October 17, October 12–14
Best Days for Love: October 6, October 22
Best Days for Money: October 8–9, October 23–24
Best Days for Career: October 3, October 21
Lucky Color: Charcoal gray – For grounded courage, truth-telling, and protection through transition

Affirmation for October:
"I release what no longer serves me. I trust the unknown. I rise as who I truly am."

Ritual: Crossroads Clarity

This ritual is designed to help Aries integrate the intense transformation of October by naming what must go, honoring what's unfolding, and claiming their next version.

You'll Need:

- Two candles (black and white or gray and red)
- A journal
- A safe space without interruption

Steps:

1. Light both candles. Sit quietly and take 3 grounding breaths.
2. On one journal page, write: *"I release..."* and list all roles, fears, patterns, or relationships that no longer align. Be honest.
3. On a new page, write: *"I choose..."* and declare the qualities, values, or new identity you are stepping into.
4. Read both pages aloud. Then fold the "release" page and burn or safely discard it.
5. Sit with the "choose" page. Reread it daily until the end of the month. It is your new compass.

Ritual Mantra:
"I honor what was. I choose what will be. I trust who I'm becoming."

Journaling Prompts for October

Use these to process emotions, decisions, and eclipses:

- What is ending for me, even if I didn't choose it?
- What old identity am I afraid to let go of?
- Where am I ready to choose myself with no apology?
- Who am I becoming—and how can I support that version of me?

Return to these during the week of October 17 for powerful insight.

Final Words for October

Dear Aries, this is not the month to fight for control. This is the month to **surrender with intention**.

October doesn't just nudge change—it demands it. The old version of you, the one built on survival, proving, pleasing, or pushing, is done. Eclipses have cracked the shell.

Now, you stand in a clearing. Not empty, but full of possibility.

Some doors will close this month. Others will slam. Some people will leave, and some truths will land like thunder. But through it all, you're being carved back to your essence—not your performance.

You are not here to repeat the past.

You are here to rise, raw and ready, into your future.

Let October wash away what's false. Let what remains be unmistakably, fiercely you.

November: Deep Dive Decisions

Welcome to November, Aries. After October's eclipses shook loose the past, this month delivers one message: **"Choose wisely, and choose deeply."**

Scorpio season intensifies your inner world—bringing emotions, motivations, and commitments to the surface. This isn't a month for guesswork. It's a time for **discernment**, **emotional honesty**, and **long-range vision**. Every move you make now echoes into your future.

With your ruling planet, Mars, entering Scorpio on **November 5**, your energy shifts from impulsive to precise. You don't want noise—you want **truth**. Your power this month lies not in doing more, but in going deeper: deeper into relationships, purpose, and your psyche.

This is the month to:

- Finalize what October revealed
- Cut emotional or energetic cords still draining you
- Invest in what sustains—not just excites—you

As the year winds down, November becomes a pivot point. It's where you stop reacting—and start **strategically choosing**.

Overview Theme: Deep Dive Decisions

October asked you to let go. November asks: *Now what?*

Scorpio season brings no fluff. It wants your full attention, emotional honesty, and willingness to **transform**. It rules intimacy, shared power, and psychological depth. You'll feel called to get real—not just with others, but with yourself.

This is a time for:

- Closing energetic and emotional loops
- Facing truth over comfort
- Making bold, soul-rooted choices

The most powerful date this month is **November 5**, when Mars enters Scorpio—your ruler, moving into a fellow warrior sign. You'll feel sharper, quieter, and more strategic. No more rushing in. You're now playing **long game energy**.

By **November 15–18**, expect insight and emotional clarity to peak. Decisions you've been dancing around may now become non-negotiable. And instead of feeling heavy, these choices will feel like *freedom.*

Key message: *"Where focus goes, energy flows. Choose with your future in mind."*

Life Area Forecasts

Career

Your career direction becomes more focused—and more selective.

With Scorpio influence and Mars' laser precision, you'll be less interested in being busy and more invested in **meaningful, strategic work**. This is a powerful time to:

- Reassess long-term goals
- Deepen your expertise or niche
- Rebuild your professional identity around truth, not trends

November 5–20 is ideal for:

- Confidential negotiations or contracts
- Rebranding or redefining your mission
- Taking bold steps toward a more fulfilling career path

But here's the truth: If you've been clinging to roles, routines, or reputations that no longer reflect your growth, this month may feel confronting. You'll be asked to **either recommit or release**.

Use Scorpio's penetrating energy to ask:

- "What am I no longer willing to pretend I want?"

- “Where am I overdelivering with little return?”
- “What version of success aligns with my life now?”

This month doesn’t reward performance. It rewards purpose.

Power Tip: You don’t need to be everywhere. You need to be **fully present** in what matters.

Money

Money becomes a mirror this month—reflecting both your relationship with control and your willingness to choose **long-term sustainability over short-term pleasure**.

Scorpios rule shared finances, debt, investments, and energetic exchange. You’ll be nudged to:

- Review financial partnerships (personal or business)
- Examine emotional spending or under-earning patterns
- Set boundaries around money, energy, or unpaid labor

November 10–14 is a good time to renegotiate terms, consolidate debt, or revise savings plans. You may also become more aware of what “energetic reciprocity” looks like in your financial life:

- Are you overgiving time or value without return?
- Are you tied to income streams that deplete your well-being?
- Is your pricing or salary in line with your true worth?

Let Scorpio season guide you to a money model that reflects your values—not just your fears.

Power Tip: True wealth feels safe, aligned, and sovereign.

Love – Singles

Aries, love gets deep, magnetic, and emotionally charged this November. But with Scorpio in the air, this isn't the month for casual flirtation—it's a season of **soul-level truth and vulnerability**.

If you're dating or seeking connection, prepare for encounters that challenge your defenses. With **Mars in Scorpio from November 5**, your desire intensifies—but so does your awareness of what's real versus what's performative.

You may find yourself:

- Attracted to someone who triggers your healing
- Revisiting an old pattern you thought was complete

- Faced with a choice between emotional depth and easy chemistry

This month doesn't promise fairy-tale romance. But it offers **intimacy with integrity**—if you're willing to be fully seen.

Watch for **November 11–17**, when a heart-opening conversation or realization may prompt a shift in your approach to love. Don't be afraid to speak your truth, even if it feels raw. That's where real connection lives.

Power Tip: Magnetism is great. But mutual emotional availability? That's where the magic is.

Love – Couples

For partnered Aries, November is all about **emotional honesty and shared power**. Scorpio energy doesn't tolerate surface-level engagement. If something's been simmering beneath the surface, it will rise now—ready to be addressed, healed, or cleared.

Themes you might face:

- Power imbalances or control issues
- Fear of vulnerability or loss
- Questions around emotional or financial trust

This isn't necessarily a crisis month—but it is a **truth month**. Especially between **November 8–15**, conversations may feel intense—but they hold the potential for **breakthroughs** if approached with compassion and curiosity.

Ask yourselves:

- Are we truly seeing and supporting each other?
- Are we avoiding a conversation we both need?
- Is our foundation built on fear, duty, or desire?

Some couples will find this a powerful moment to deepen their bond. Others may recognize it's time to lovingly part ways. Both outcomes are valid—Scorpio doesn't care about appearances. It wants **truth**.

Power Tip: Real intimacy doesn't require perfection. It requires presence.

Health

Your physical and emotional health are deeply intertwined this month, Aries. The eclipse hangover is real, and Scorpio energy draws your attention inward—especially toward **emotional stress stored in the body**.

This is the time to support:

- Your **nervous system** (through grounding, rest, and reducing overstimulation)
- Your **digestion** (Scorpio rules elimination—emotional and physical)

- Your **emotional hygiene** (clear out repressed emotions, not just your inbox)

Good practices this month:

- Energy healing or therapy
- Emotional release journaling or breathwork
- Trauma-informed movement (yoga, qigong, gentle stretching)

Be especially kind to your body between **November 5–12**, when Mars enters Scorpio and amplifies both your power and your pressure. Don't overdo it. Rest is strategic now.

Also, protect your energy. Scorpio season can bring up psychic clutter. Clean your space. Take social media breaks. Say no to emotional dumping grounds.

Power Tip: You don't need to do more. You need to **feel safe** where you are.

Astro Summary Box: November at a Glance

Best Days Overall: November 6–8, November 18–20
Most Stressful Days Overall: November 3–4, November 14–15
Best Days for Love: November 11, November 20
Best Days for Money: November 10, November 22
Best Days for Career: November 6, November 17–18

Lucky Color: Dark burgundy – For depth, power, and anchored purpose

Affirmation for November:
"I choose with clarity. I commit with courage. I create from truth."

Ritual: The Clarity Compass

This ritual helps you navigate important choices by aligning action with intuition and long-term truth.

You'll Need:

- A candle (dark red or white)
- 1 sheet of paper and a pen
- 10–15 minutes of uninterrupted quiet

Steps:

1. Light your candle. Sit quietly with one hand over your heart.
2. On your paper, draw a large compass with four quadrants. Label them:
    - **Mind** – What makes logical sense?
    - **Heart** – What do I truly want?
    - **Body** – What feels right in my gut?
    - **Soul** – What aligns with who I'm becoming?
3. Choose a situation or decision you're sitting with.
4. For each quadrant, write 2–3 thoughts or insights.

5. Close by writing your "Clarity Statement": *"I choose ______ because it aligns with my mind, heart, body, and soul."*

Keep your compass somewhere visible this month. Return to it when in doubt.

Journaling Prompts for November

Use these to explore your emotional truth, power, and readiness to commit:

- What have I outgrown—and what do I need to stop pretending works?
- Where am I afraid to commit, and why?
- What part of me still needs healing before I choose clearly?
- Who am I becoming, and what decisions support that version of me?

These prompts are especially potent between **November 12–20**.

Final Words for November

Aries, October cracked you open. November now asks you to **choose with intention**.

The fire inside you is refining—not roaring. You're no longer chasing every spark. You're aiming your flame with focus. That's what real power is.

Let this month be the one where you:

- Say yes with clarity
- Say no without guilt
- Invest only in what feeds your future

You don't need a perfect plan. You need an **honest one**. Built from your full self—not your fear.

This is the moment to trust that inner knowing. The version of you that's whispering beneath the noise?

She's ready.

December: Sacred Integration

December isn't asking you to hustle, Aries. It's asking you to **exhale**.

After a year of bold action, emotional release, and intense transformation, you've reached a quieter chapter—but no less meaningful. This month is about **integration**—the sacred pause that allows the lessons of 2026 to sink in, stabilize, and settle into your bones.

The month begins in expansive **Sagittarius energy**, which invites you to zoom out and reconnect with your *why*. This is the philosophical fire—less about impulse, more about vision. You may find yourself drawn to books, wisdom teachers, spiritual conversations, or solo travel. Not to escape—but to gain **clarity and closure**.

By **mid-December**, Capricorn season arrives, grounding the fire with earth. Now you're asked to turn that vision into quiet preparation. This is the season of root work: tending your foundation, protecting your energy, and releasing anything that doesn't belong in 2027.

Key message: *"You don't need to do more. You need to honor what's already transformed."*

Overview Theme: Sacred Integration

Imagine a traveler returning from a long, wild expedition. Their bags are full, their shoes are worn, and their heart are heavy with stories. But before they rush to their next journey, they must **rest, unpack, and reflect**.

That's where you are now, Aries.

December is not a launchpad. It's a landing zone.

It's the moment you:

- Digest the emotional intensity of eclipse season
- Realize how much you've grown—even when it didn't feel like it
- Prepare emotionally and spiritually for a new cycle

Sagittarius energy until **December 20** helps you take inventory:

- What did 2026 teach you about yourself?
- What stories are you ready to release—or rewrite?
- What truth did you finally stop denying?

Then, Capricorn energy moves in—urging simplicity, structure, and sacred solitude. Think: fewer social obligations, more evenings journaling. Fewer "goals," more quiet **alignment**.

This is not a void. This is a **holy reset**.

Life Area Forecasts

Career

In December, your work life softens—not because it's unimportant, but because you're being asked to zoom out and realign.

With Mercury retrograde beginning mid-month (**December 13–January 2**), this is *not* the time to launch something major, sign long-term contracts, or push productivity out of panic. Instead:

- Reflect on what worked—and what didn't—in 2026
- Revisit your long-term vision
- Permit yourself to rest without guilt

Between **December 7–10**, insights may come through conversations, dreams, or sudden flashes of clarity. Take note—but don't force action. Capricorn season supports quiet recalibration over loud achievement.

Ask yourself:

- Am I still aligned with the direction I chose at the start of the year?
- What kind of work supports my nervous system and purpose?
- How can I prepare—not push—for 2027?

This month favors **creative strategy**, spiritual alignment, and clearing workspaces (digital and physical). Make room for what's next by cleaning out what's expired.

Power Tip: Trust that stillness now creates momentum later.

Money

Your financial energy in December reflects the overall theme: **clear, simple, intentional**.

This isn't the time to make impulsive purchases or high-risk moves. With Mercury retrograde in the mix, financial clarity comes through review—not reinvention.

Use the first two weeks of the month to:

- Check in on subscriptions, debts, and savings
- Create (or revisit) a values-based budget for 2027
- Consider donating or giving in a way that feels spiritually aligned

If financial anxiety creeps up during the Capricorn shift, pause. Ask yourself: *Is this fear or intuition?* Capricorn energy wants structure—not scarcity. You may feel called to simplify your spending, not out of restriction, but out of a desire for **peace**.

Ideal window for financial planning or gentle resets: **December 8–12**

Avoid major investments or tech purchases from **December 13–January 2**, while Mercury retrogrades.

Power Tip: You don't need more—just more *clarity* about what truly matters.

Love – Singles

For single Aries, December offers peace, not pressure.

After a year of romantic revelations, intensity, and emotional re-patterning, this month brings a welcome slowdown. The fire of Sagittarius season may stoke some curiosity or a desire for soulful conversation, but you're not likely to chase love in the old, impulsive ways.

Instead, your energy softens into something more **receptive**, more reflective.

December invites you to ask:

- "What kind of relationship supports the person I'm becoming?"
- "What emotional residue am I still carrying from past patterns or people?"
- "Do I need romance—or rest?"

Don't be surprised if you feel more introverted than usual. Or if solitude suddenly feels delicious. That's sacred. Honor it.

Between **December 10–20**, old emotions may rise—not to hurt you, but to help you release. Especially if someone from your past reappears in a dream, text, or memory. Don't fall back—*fall inward.*

Power Tip: If it doesn't bring peace to your nervous system, it's not love—it's repetition.

Love – Couples

For couples, December is about **emotional co-regulation, mutual reflection, and quiet intimacy**.

This is not the month for big relationship decisions. It's a time to sit beside each other and say: *"Wow, we've made it through a lot."*

Let go of the need to solve, fix, or force. Use this month to:

- Create shared rituals of stillness (tea before bed, tech-free dinners, daily gratitude)
- Revisit dreams you planted earlier in the year
- Ask each other gentle questions, like:
    - "What did we learn this year as a couple?"
    - "What helped us feel closest?"
    - "Where do we want to go next—together?"

Sagittarius season (until **Dec 20**) can bring back shared vision. Capricorn season brings grounding. Use both.

And if things have been rocky, don't push. Don't force clarity. Let Mercury retrograde (starting **Dec 13**) slow things down so you can hear your *real* feelings—not just reactive ones.

Power Tip: Presence is more intimate than words. Just be there, fully.

Health

You've made it through a high-voltage year—and your body knows it.

December is the month to let your **nervous system decompress**, your sleep deepen, and your energy **reset**.

Physical healing is best supported by:

- Gentle movement (slow yoga, walking, stretching)
- Deep hydration and whole foods
- Tech breaks and sleep hygiene

Emotional and spiritual healing is just as important. Dreamwork becomes more vivid. Memories may resurface—not to haunt you, but to give you the chance to **reprocess from a safer place**.

Give yourself:

- More baths, less urgency
- More journaling, less scrolling
- More silence, less stimulation

December 12–22 is ideal for spiritual clearing, somatic sessions, or any practice that reconnects you to the deeper wisdom of your body.

Don't mistake rest for regression. You are not "falling behind." You're **recalibrating** for the next season of your life.

Power Tip: The most sacred work sometimes looks like... doing nothing.

Astro Summary Box: December at a Glance

Best Days Overall: December 4–6, December 21–22
Most Stressful Days Overall: December 12–15, December 26–28
Best Days for Love: December 11, December 20
Best Days for Money: December 8, December 18
Best Days for Career: December 6, December 22
Lucky Color: Sage green – For healing, reflection, and spiritual renewal

Affirmation for December:
"I rest. I receive. I remember who I am becoming."

Ritual: Year-End Integration

This ritual helps Aries process and honor the growth of 2026—and cross into 2027 with peace, clarity, and self-trust.

You'll Need:

- Candle (white or soft gold)
- Paper + pen
- Bowl of water
- 30 minutes of quiet

Steps:

1. Light your candle and sit comfortably. Close your eyes. Take three deep breaths.
2. Write this sentence at the top of your page:
   "2026 taught me..."
   Then list everything that comes to mind—big and small.
3. Fold that list and place it beside you.
4. On a new page, write: *"In 2027, I choose..."*
   Write what you're inviting in—values, energies, priorities.
5. Dip your fingers into the water. Say aloud:
   "I cleanse the past. I carry only wisdom forward."
6. Blow out the candle slowly, in gratitude.

Optional: Burn or bury your "2026" page after reading it one last time.

Journaling Prompts for December

Use these to close your year with presence and power:

- What am I most proud of from this year?
- What lesson hurt the most—and taught me the most?
- Where did I reclaim my power?
- What do I want less of next year?
- What do I want more of—and am I willing to receive it?

Return to these between **December 22–31**, as Capricorn season anchors you.

Final Words for December

Dear Aries, your fire has burned bright this year.

You've lit up new paths, burned bridges that needed to fall, and stood inside your storms with bravery. But now, the flame softens. Not extinguished—just quieter. Warmer. Wiser.

December doesn't want more effort from you. It wants your **presence**. It wants you to sit in the richness of what's already been done. Already overcome. Already *become*.

Let yourself be held by the stillness. Let yourself trust that you don't need to push to be powerful. The truth is, you never did.

Next year is coming. But you're not late. You're not behind. You're exactly where your soul needs you to be.

This is sacred ground.

About the Author

Lyra M. Rising is a cosmic guide, intuitive writer, and lifelong student of the stars. With a background in symbolic systems, mythology, and esoteric astrology, she weaves together timeless wisdom and modern soulwork to help others reclaim their inner fire.

Her work bridges astrology with emotional healing, seasonal alignment, and self-leadership—especially for those walking the path of deep transformation. She believes that horoscopes are not predictions, but portals: invitations to live more consciously, courageously, and soulfully.

When she's not writing under moonlight or reading natal charts, Lyra can be found journaling in quiet cafés, watching the sky shift colors, and tending to her rituals of becoming.

Aries Horoscope & Soul Guide for 2026 is the first in her 12-sign series, offering a sacred companion for those ready to meet each month with presence, power, and purpose.

www.ingramcontent.com/pod-product-compliance
Lightning Source LLC
Chambersburg PA
CBHW021918020426
42352CB00009B/168
* 9 7 9 8 2 3 1 1 9 6 7 2 2 *